HEAVEN, HELL, AND BEYOND

JOHN MARINELLI

Heaven, Hell & Beyond
Copyright © 2020 John Marinelli
Ocala, Florida …All rights reserved.

First Edition: 2023
Print ISBN: 978-1-08-808887-6
eBook ISBN: 978-1-08-808888-3

Cover and Formatting: Streetlight Graphics
Contact: johnmarinelli@embarqmail.com

This book is protected under US copyright laws. Any reproduction or other use is prohibited without the written permission of the author.

No part of this book may be reproduced, scanned, or distributed in any printed or electronic form without permission. Please do not participate in or encourage piracy of copyrighted materials in violation of the author's rights. Thank you for respecting the hard work of this author.

TABLE OF CONTENTS

Preface	v
Introduction	vii
Chapter One: Is Heaven Real?	1
Chapter Two: Does Hell Really Exist?	21
Chapter Three: Beyond Heaven And Hell	60
Chapter Four: How To Be "Born Again"	65
Conclusion	77
About The Author John Marinelli	78
Gallery of Encouraging Christian Poems	79

PREFACE

This book is focused on heaven, hell and what comes next. We will be looking at trends as to beliefs in the reality of hell and a real place called heaven. We will also consider what comes next, after all is said and done.

We will look into the premise that holds true to where we go after death and why we go there. All resource materials are from the Bible and noted authors or bloggers.

My goal in publishing "Heaven, Hell and Beyond" is to call attention to the reality of after death destinations and life or death situations that may await the dying soul.

INTRODUCTION

Most of us live life as though it will never end. However, the world-wide death rate proves us wrong. The death rate exceeds 150,000 deaths per day. Here are some stats from the WorldPopulationReview.com reports:

Deaths per Day: **183,671.**

Deaths per Hour: **7,653.**

Deaths per Minute: 128.

Deaths per Second: 2.13.

We are all going to die one day. Some sooner than later. Some unexpectedly and others due to old age or a host of other causes. When it's your time to die, you, like more than 150,000 that die every day, will leave this earth and off you go. But to where?

Some folks believe that they will be reincarnated and come back as a cow or a different person through a process called transmigration of the soul. Others feel that they will just cease to exist. Then there are those that have no opinion. They just avoid the issue and hope for the best.

I believe in the Bible. It says that there is a final judgement and an eternal destiny for every soul. This is part of the core values of the Christian faith.

The Bible also says that there is a heaven and a hell and a life beyond death. It tells us that there is a road that leads to eternal life and another road the leads to eternal damnation. Let's take a look at the scriptures and learn what God wants us to know.

CHAPTER ONE:

IS HEAVEN REAL?

I would say yes. However, the Bible actually speaks of three heavens.

The word Heaven is found seven times in the first chapter of the Bible alone. It is the seventh word into the Bible. In Genesis 1, we see that it means more than the Celestial City.

The First Heaven... is spoken of twenty-one times in the Bible. It is where the atmosphere is and where we see blue skies, clouds and birds. The Bible speaks of the birds or fowls of the "air." For example: Psalm 104:12, "By them shall the fowls of the heaven have their habitation, which sing among the branches." The "Dew of Heaven" is mentioned nine times. One example is Genesis 27:28,

"Therefore, God give thee of the dew of heaven, and the fatness of the earth, and plenty of corn and wine:" The 1st heaven is commonly referred to as the firmament which means "expanse or sky." (Genesis 1:8)

The Second Heaven... is where the stars and planets are. We would refer to it as "Outer Space." Here are a few scriptures that refer to the 2nd heaven:

1. Genesis 1: 14-17, "And God said, let there be lights in the firmament of the heaven to divide the day from the night; and let them be for signs, and for seasons, and for days, and years: And let them be for lights in the firmament of the heaven to give light upon the earth: and it was so. And God made two great lights; the greater light to rule the day, and the lesser light to rule the night: he made the stars also. And God set them

in the firmament of the heaven to give light upon the earth." The phrase "stars of heaven" occurs eleven times in scripture.

2. Isaiah 13:10, "For the stars of heaven and the constellations thereof shall not give their light: the sun shall be darkened in his going forth, and the moon shall not cause her light to shine."

3. Psalm 8:3, 4, "When I consider thy heavens, the work of thy fingers, the moon and the stars, which thou hast ordained; what is man, that thou art mindful of him? and the son of man, that thou visit him?"

4. Psalm 19:1, "The heavens declare the glory of God; and the firmament shews his handiwork."

The Third Heaven... is the current heaven where God dwells. Although this is a glorious place, this is not the New Heaven described in Revelation 21 and 22. It is far above the sky and our entire known universe. It is a physical place that is full of angels, saints, animals, and much more.

Paul went to the third heaven and came back. (II Corinthians 12:2-4.) "I knew a man in Christ above fourteen years ago, whether in the body, I cannot tell; or whether out of the body, I cannot tell: God knows; such an one caught up to the third heaven. And I knew such a man, whether in the body, or out of the body, I cannot tell: God knows; how that he was caught up into paradise, and heard unspeakable words, which it is not lawful for a man to utter."

Isaiah saw a glimpse of heaven. (Isaiah 6:1-7), "In the year that king Uzziah died I saw also the Lord sitting upon a throne, high and lifted up, and his train filled the temple.

Above it stood the seraphims: each one had six wings; with twain he covered his face, and with twain he covered his feet, and with twain he did fly. And one cried unto another, and said, holy, holy, holy, is the LORD of hosts: the whole earth is full of his glory. And the posts of the door moved at the voice of him that cried, and the house was filled with smoke.

Then said I, Woe is me! for I am undone; because I am a man of unclean lips, and I dwell in the midst of a people of unclean lips: for mine eyes have seen the King, the LORD of hosts.

Then flew one of the seraphims unto me, having a live coal in his hand, which he had taken with the tongs from off the altar: And he laid it upon my mouth, and said, Lo, this hath touched thy lips; and thine iniquity is taken away, and thy sin purged."

This text reveals several things about the third heaven:

- The Lord is sitting upon a throne
- The Lord is wearing a robe with a very long train (hem).
- There is a temple in Heaven where he sits.
- Six winged seraphims ceaselessly fly above the throne of God and cry one to another announcing the holiness of the Lord of Hosts.
- There is an altar of live coals. John also saw the third heaven and penned the book of Revelation. Here are a few observations:
- There is a door in Heaven (4:1). The door is opened to all who hear the first audible voice and the sound of the trumpet.
- There is a throne set in Heaven. It is the same one Isaiah saw (Isaiah 4:2).
- God who sits on the throne is described as being like jasper (clear crystal) and a sardine stone (dark red). This was the best way John could describe God's glory (4:3).
- There is a rainbow about the throne (4:3). Our rainbows on earth are made of red, orange, yellow, green, blue, indigo, and violet. This one appears as an emerald, which is green. Green represents life.
- Around God's throne are twenty-four seats. There are twenty-four elders, clothed in white raiment, sitting on the seats. They wear crowns of gold (4:4). For a full list of what the book of Revelation discloses as being in the third heaven, visit http://www.fbbc.com/messages/kohl_doctrine_ouranology.html and read Art Kohl's article.

One day these three heavens will no longer exist. (Isaiah 65:17) "For, behold, I create new heavens and a new earth: and the former shall not be remembered, nor come into mind."

We do not know what the new heavens will look like but we will see a heaven on earth where Jesus is King and we will reign with him. We shall dwell with him, on the new earth, forever. John 14:1-4 records Jesus telling his followers that there were many mansions in his Father's house.

He even said that he would not have told them if it were not so. I do believe that God has a house/place where he dwells and it is full of redeemed saints, angels and lots more. If we die before Jesus returns, we will see it and dwell there too until we take that glorious ride on heavenly horseback through time and space with Jesus at his 2nd coming.

Now that we know that heaven is a real place. The next discovery is to find out who was it prepared for? Does everybody go to heaven when they die? If so, it is a busy place with over 150,000 arrivals every day.

You cannot talk about heaven without including hell because people go there as well. We will discuss hell in chapter two. For now, it is reasonable to conclude that of the 150,000 deaths per day, many will not arrive in heaven but will go straight to hell.

Those that make it to heaven will experience the glory of God as they enter into his presence.

We all know this life will come to an end. Whether you're coping with the loss of a loved one or have questions about your own mortality and the hereafter, these answers on heaven from Billy Graham may help.

Q: What happens to us in the first minute after we die? Do we enter heaven immediately, or do our souls go into some kind of soul sleep?

The Bible doesn't answer all our questions about heaven and life after death—and the reason is because our minds are limited and heaven is far too glorious for us to understand. Someday, all of our questions will be answered—but not yet. As the Apostle Paul wrote, "Now I know in part; then I shall know fully" (1 Corinthians 13:12).

However, the Bible certainly does indicate that when we die we enter immediately into God's presence if we belong to Christ. From our earthly point of view, death looks somewhat like sleep—but not from God's point of view.

Paul declared, "We are confident (of eternal life), I say, and would prefer to be away from the body and at home with the Lord" (2 Corinthians 5:8). Elsewhere he wrote, "I desire to depart and be with Christ, which is better by far" (Philippians 1:23).

Later, we will be given new bodies—bodies that will never age or be subject to death, because they will be like Christ's resurrection body. As the Bible says, "The dead will be raised imperishable, and we will be changed" (1 Corinthians 15:52).

Q: Will we recognize our loved ones in heaven? Will they recognize us?

I have no doubt that in heaven your mother will recognize you, and you will recognize her—even if you never knew each other on earth. When King David's infant son died, David declared, "I will go to him" (2 Samuel 12:23).

Perhaps you are thinking of Isaiah 65:17: "Behold, I will create new heavens and a new earth. The former things will not be remembered, nor will they come to mind." But this verse has nothing to do with whether or not we will be reunited with our loved ones in heaven if we know Christ. Instead, it gives us a great promise: Someday all the sins and pains and failures of this world will be over, and we will be with Christ forever.

More than that, God has promised that in heaven nothing—even the memory of this world's sin and pain—will cast a shadow over the joy he has in store for us. Think about that for a moment. In this world, even the memory of what someone did to us years ago can still cause us pain. But that won't be true in heaven, because our focus won't be on the past but on Christ and what he means to us.

In the meantime, make it your goal to walk with Jesus every day. Do you know him? If not, make your commitment to him today. Then take comfort in his promise: "I am going there (to heaven) to prepare a place for you" (John 14:2).

Q: When we get to heaven, will we know what's happening on earth? If so, how can we be happy with all the misery in the world?

The Bible doesn't answer all our questions about heaven—and we don't know exactly how much knowledge those in heaven have about what happens here. The Bible does say that "we are surrounded by ... a great cloud of witnesses" (i.e., those who have already entered heaven) but it isn't clear if this means they are able to observe our lives (Hebrews 12:1).

But what we do know about heaven is that we will be with God—and because of that, heaven is a place of supreme joy. The Bible says, "You will fill me with joy in your presence, with eternal pleasures at your right hand" (Psalm 16:11). And even if we do see something of what is happening on earth, we'll see the whole picture then, and we'll realize how it all fits in with God's eternal plan. We'll realize too that evil and death will be defeated, and Christ will be victorious. That will give us joy!

Heaven is the heritage of every believer—because Christ conquered Death and Hell and Satan by his resurrection from the dead. Have you put your faith and trust in him for your salvation? Make sure of your eternal destiny by turning to Christ in repentance and faith, and committing your life to him.

Then ask God to use you to encourage others who are overwhelmed by life's burdens. Yes, our world is full of misery—but God wants to use you to point others to Christ, who alone can give us hope and new life.

Q: Does an angel accompany us into heaven when we die?

Yes, the Bible indicates that when believers die, the angels will escort them safely into heaven.

In one of his parables, for example, Jesus talked about two very different men. One was a rich man, who lived only for himself and ignored both God and others. The other was a poor beggar who had nothing as far as this world's goods were concerned, but had faith in God and his promises. When the rich man died, he received what he deserved: a life of misery, separated from God forever. But when the poor man died, the angels accompanied him safely into God's presence. (You can read this parable in Luke 16:19-31.)

Although we may not see them or even be aware of their presence, God's angels are real, and when we know Christ, we know they are always with us to safeguard us from Satan's attacks. If they safeguard us now, can't they also be trusted to safeguard our journey to heaven? Of course. The Bible says, "Are not all angels ministering spirits sent to serve those who will inherit salvation?" (Hebrews 1:14).

Never forget, however, that Christ alone is our Savior, and he alone is the one in whom we are to place our faith and trust. We should be grateful for God's angels, but we are not to worship them or make them (instead of Christ) the center of our faith. Is Christ the center of your faith? Make sure of your commitment to him. Then put your confidence in God's promise: "For he will command his angels concerning you to guard you in all your ways" (Psalm 91:11).

Q: Will there be animals in heaven?

Heaven will be a place of perfect happiness for us—and if we need animals around us to make our happiness complete, then you can be sure God will have them there.

Heaven will be glorious—far beyond anything we can fully imagine. It will be glorious first of all because it will be perfect. All the sufferings, conflicts and disappointments of this life will be over, and death will no longer exist. Sin will be banished, and Satan will never again have any influence over our lives. One of the Bible's greatest promises declares,

"There will be no more death or mourning or crying or pain, for the old order of things has passed away" (Revelation 21:4).

But heaven will be glorious most of all because we'll be in the presence of God and of Jesus Christ. Even the most glorious thing we can imagine on earth or in the heavens is but a pale reflection of the glory of God. Think of it: If you know Christ, some day you will be with him forever!

But the Bible also promises that at the end of time God will bring about a new heaven and a new earth (see 2 Peter 3:13). We will share in that wondrous world, and in that day, many scholars believe, the Bible's prophecy will be fulfilled: "The wolf will live with the lamb. ... And the lion will eat straw like the ox" (Isaiah 11:6-7). **Find more helpful answers in *The Heaven Answer Book* by Billy Graham.**

Author's Note" Animals In The Resurrection

How many of us have lost a companion animal? We grieve for them as they were human and we even write poetry about them as a continual remembrance of their companionship. Marilyn, my wife, and I have lost several companion animals over the years. If you are an animal lover, you will understand and appreciate our viewpoint. It answers the question that torments most of us that can only watch as our companion animals die.

Do They Go To Heaven?

There is a big controversy over whether or not our beloved companion animals go to heaven when they pass away. It is a tough thing to go through when your best friend dies...The one who has been there for you every day for years, waiting for you to come home, wanting to play and watching over you with a protective growl when strangers approach. Researchers say that the grieving process for a companion animal is equal to and sometimes even greater that the loss of a human family member.

We must go to the only absolute source to find the answer to the question, **"Do animals Go To Heaven When They Die"** I believe in the absolute and infallible authority of the Bible. It is here that we found peace and comfort when our first beloved companion animal died. The holy scriptures can also be a source of comfort to you in your sorrow.

The animals were created by God, (Gen 1:24), and they were placed under the dominion of Adam. (Gen 1:26) That means we are responsible for their wellbeing. How is it then that 70%-80% of all animals that enter animal shelters in the US are destroyed? Here's what the Bible says about animals and Heaven:

- The apostle Paul writes: *The creation waits in eager expectation for the sons of God to be revealed. For the creation was subjected to frustration, not by its own choice, but by the will of the one who subjected it, in hope that the creation itself will be liberated from its bondage to decay and brought into the glorious freedom of the children of God – Romans 8:1921 NIV.*

Animals, according to this scripture passage, are now subject to the vanity and Sin of man, but when the human drama is over and the children of God are revealed, all the animals that were in bondage will become partakers of that freedom.

- *And every creature which is in heaven and on the earth and under the earth and such as are in the sea, and all that are in them, I heard saying: "Blessing and honor and glory and power be to him who sits on the throne, and to the Lamb, forever and ever!" – Revelation 5:13 NKJ.*

Our companion animals will join us in praise and worship of the Lord for his glorious salvation. How great is that?

- *The wolf will live with the lamb, the leopard will lie down with the goat, the calf and the lion and the yearling together; and a little child will lead them – Isaiah 11:6 NIV.*

If the "wild" animals are going to be in heaven, then certainly our beloved pets will be there too.

You can rest assured that your beloved companion animals will go to heaven when they die, but what about you? Where will you spend eternity?

As I explained, the animals are subject to the vanity of man and are under that bondage until the children of God are revealed at the end of the human drama. We, on the other hand, are in bondage to Sin and subject to our own choices in life. Here's what the Bible says about that:

- "As it is written, there is none righteous, no, not one: There is none that understands, there is none that seeks after God. They are all gone out of the way, they are altogether become unprofitable; there is none that doeth good, no, not one." (Romans 3-10-12)
- "For all have sinned, and come short of the glory of God" (Romans 3:23)
- "For the wages of sin is death; but the gift of God is eternal life through Jesus Christ our Lord." (Romans 6:23)
- "Wherefore, as by one man, sin entered into the world, and death by sin; and so death passed upon all men, for that all have sinned" (Romans 5:12-14)

These simple Scripture passages tell us that we have fallen short of God's Glory. Man's fall from Glory came as a result of disobedience, which is considered Sin. The penalty for sin is death, which passed upon all men, because all have sinned.

- No one can say they are righteous. We do not seek God. Instead, he seeks us and we respond to his love from a repentant heart. Jesus said, "No man can come to me except my Father draw him first" (John 6:44) He also said, "For God so loved the world that He gave His only begotten Son, that whosoever, believes in Him, should not perish but have everlasting life" (John 3:16)

We have the privilege to believe in Jesus as God's only Son, who was given as a sacrifice for sin, our sins, so we could escape the sentence of death and live forever with God, as it was originally planned.

The word "Salvation" means to be delivered. To be saved is to be delivered from the fear of death. It becomes a reality when we personally accept Jesus as our Savior, agreeing with God, that all, including us, have fallen short and are in need of his redemption.

Our companion animals will see God and dwell with him throughout all eternity. A simple prayer of repentance and a cry to God for salvation can secure our destiny and assure us that we will see our "Best Friends" again.

Who Lives In Heaven

Heaven was and still is where God dwells. It is also where the angels reside. It is currently being prepared for the children of God. They are those that were, "Born Again" while on earth. We will discuss this in more detail in chapter four. Now, heaven is being filled with the redeemed.

A Remnant Equals a Few

Consider this; the Bible says that only a remnant will be saved. (Romans 9:27) Webster says that a remnant is "a small remaining quantity of something." We do not know how many are in a remnant but I am sure it is not very much. Here's why!

A small remaining quantity is left after God destroys everything. Some folks say a small quantity is about 2%. If we do the math, 2% of 150,000 that die every hour will equal 3,000. However, God does not save those that reject him and his plan of salvation. The 3,000 would be an average and may be even less depending on the free will choices of those that died.

Jesus put it this way, "Enter ye in at the strait gate: for wide is the gate, and broad is the way, that leadeth to destruction, and many there be which go in thereat: because strait is the gate, and narrow is the way, which leadeth unto life, and few there be that find it" Matthew 7:13-14

Few is the same as remnant…*a small number of:*

The point is…we need to be sure that we are entering in at the straight gate (Jesus) and are walking the narrow path. That sets us apart from the crowd and their expectations. We live for Jesus and walk in his footsteps.

"Wherefore come out from among them, and be ye separate, saith the Lord, and touch not the unclean thing; and I will receive you." 2 Corinthians 6:17

Some Questions To Consider (From Gotquestions.org)

Will Heaven Be on Earth?

"heaven" is not the final destination for believers in Christ. In the Old Testament, *heaven* usually refers to "the heavens," that is, the sky or maybe what we would call space—some place "up there."

This came to be associated with where God is. In Revelation, we see worship of God taking place in heaven (chapters 4—5), but the word *heaven* can also refer to "the sky." When Jesus ascended, he ascended "into heaven" (Acts 1:11), but this may simply mean that he went up, without specifying that he went to a place called heaven. Likewise, when he returns, he will descend from heaven (1 Thessalonians 4:16). In 2 Corinthians 12,

Paul relates the experience of being caught up into the "third heaven," which is the very abode of God. Likewise, Hebrews speaks of Jesus' ministry in heaven (Hebrews 1:3; 8:1; 9:24–25). Since 2 Corinthians 5:8 says that if believers are "away from the body," that is, dead, they are "at home with the Lord," then it is accurate to say that a Christian who dies "goes to heaven."

However, heaven is not the eternal home of the Christian. Second Corinthians 5 also points out that while in heaven, away from the body, we look forward to our resurrection body. Too often, eternity with God is pictured as sitting on clouds and playing harps. Human beings were created with physical bodies, and those who have become children of God by faith in Christ are waiting for new physical, material bodies. We also know that the current heavens and earth (as referred to in Genesis 1:1) will be destroyed and replaced with new heavens and a new earth "where righteousness dwells" (2 Peter 3:12–13).

The new heavens and earth are the eternal home for the believer. The imagery in Revelation 21—22 seems to point to Eden-like conditions. Once again God will dwell among his people. Adam and Eve were given the job of tending the garden and subduing the earth before the fall, and there is every reason to believe that the people of God who inhabit the new earth in resurrection bodies will continue the work of Adam and Eve before the fall, enjoying the work they do and the unhindered fellowship with God. On the new earth, we will continue to work, learn, grow, develop, and accomplish things. Since there were animals in Eden, there may very well be animals on the new earth as well.

Revelation 21:1–5 records this scene: "Then I saw 'a new heaven and a new earth,' for the first heaven and the first earth had passed away, and there was no longer any sea. I saw the Holy City, the new Jerusalem, coming down out of heaven from God, prepared as a bride beautifully dressed for her husband. And I heard a loud voice from the throne saying, 'Look! God's dwelling place is now among the people, and he will dwell with them.

They will be his people, and God himself will be with them and be their God. "He will wipe every tear from their eyes. There will be no more death" or mourning or crying or pain, for the old order of things has passed away.' He who was seated on the throne said, *"I am making everything new!"*

It is important to note that heaven comes to earth only through God's miraculous intervention and re-creation. No amount of human effort, as noble is it may be in some cases, will ever be able to create "heaven on earth." We cannot manufacture utopia.

Through the work of the Holy Spirit, Christians have access to God and experience freedom from many of the effects of sin, but we still only have a glimpse of what is yet to come.

How Big Is Heaven?

How big is heaven—how big is the place where God lives? We know that God himself is infinite. Heaven and earth cannot contain him. In terms of time, there is no beginning or end to his years (Psalm 102:27); in terms of his kingdom, his reign will have no end (Luke 1:33); in terms of his character, He is unchanging (Hebrews 1:12; James 1:17). God created the heavens and the earth (Genesis 1:1). Of God's creation of the stars, Isaiah says, "Lift up your eyes on high and see: who created these? He who brings out their host by number, calling them all by name, by the greatness of his might, and because he is strong in power not one is missing" (Isaiah 40:26).

Scientists have not even been able to chart the size of the known physical universe. There is a photo called the XDF (eXtreme Deep Field) that was put together from images taken by the Hubble Space Telescope over the course of ten years. It shows a vast number of galaxies, each comprising billions of stars like our sun.

Our sun is 93 million miles away from the earth. And the galaxies are very, very far apart—Andromeda, the closest galaxy to our own, is 2.2 million light years away. To give an idea of how far that is, a shuttle traveling at 18,000 miles per hour would need 37,200 years to travel *one* light year. The universe is absolutely huge—and God created it all.

So, how big is heaven? We don't know exactly. The Bible doesn't give any linear measurements. When John had his vision of heaven, he wrote, "There before me was a great multitude that no one could count, from every nation, tribe, people and language, standing before the throne and before the Lamb" (Revelation 7:9). So heaven is at least big enough for the innumerable multitude—and we can assume that there will be no crowding in heaven.

Will There Literally Be Streets of Gold in Heaven?

Heaven's streets of gold are often referenced in song and poetry, but harder to find in the Bible. In fact, there is only one passage of Scripture that references streets of gold and that is in the Holy City, the New Jerusalem: "The great street of the city was of gold, as pure as transparent glass" (Revelation 21:21). So does this verse tell us that there will literally be streets of gold in heaven? And, if so, what is the importance or significance of literal streets of gold?

The Greek word translated "gold" is *chrusion*, which can mean "gold, gold jewelry, or overlay." So to translate it "gold" makes complete and perfect sense. In fact, interpreters often attempt to determine which parts of the Bible to take literally and which parts to take figuratively. A good rule of thumb when studying the Bible is to take everything literally, unless it doesn't make sense to do so. And in this chapter of Revelation, John isn't just throwing out random descriptive terms. In the early parts of Revelation 21, he is given a rod to measure out the city (verse 15), and he specifically describes the wall of heaven as being composed of jasper and the city itself also of gold (verse 18). He also describes the foundations of the city walls being comprised of many specific precious stones and jewels (verses 19–20). So, with these specifics in mind, the description of golden streets makes perfect sense in comparison to the rest of John's eyewitness description. So, if heaven's streets are made of gold, what is the point?

Notice the condition of the gold. When gold is uncovered on earth, it is not in the desirable condition that jewelers are looking for. The gold must be smelted in order that impurities float to the top for removal, leaving only the pure gold behind. The gold that John saw in heaven was of such quality that it appears to be transparent in order to reflect the pure light of God's blazing glory.

And God's ability to purify is not confined only to gold; God has purified all who will enter his heaven through the blood of Jesus Christ. "If we confess our sins, He is faithful and just to forgive us our sins and purify us from all unrighteousness" (1 John 1:9). Not only is God's holy city one of purity by His design, so are the citizens of that city.

As we investigate this idea of golden streets further, there are some teachers and scholars who do not hold to the idea that heaven's golden streets are literal. However, by looking simply at the text God has given us within the context of the entirety of John's revelation, there seems to be no reason to doubt it.

However, our attention in eternity will hardly be focused on earthly treasures. While man pursues treasures like gold on earth, one day it will simply be no more than a source of pavement for the believer in heaven. No matter how many precious jewels or materials make up the physical construction of heaven, nothing will ever be of greater value than the God who loves us and died to save us.

Are There Pearly Gates in Heaven?

The idea of there being "pearly gates" in heaven is based on a reference in the book of Revelation describing the twelve gates of New Jerusalem. The passage describes an immense and lovely city with a wall built of jasper (a kind of precious stone that can be red, yellow, brown, or green) and twelve foundations of different gemstones.

Then it describes the gates themselves: "And the twelve gates were twelve pearls, each of the gates made of a single pearl, and the street of the city was pure gold, like transparent glass" (Revelation 21:21).

In popular imagination, the "pearly gates" are often considered as the entrance into heaven, but Revelation shows the gates as belonging to the city of New Jerusalem. The city and heaven are not exactly synonymous; the city comes "down out of heaven" (Revelation 21:2) and is part of the new earth (Revelation 21:1).

Also, contrary to the popular idea that the pearly gates bar heaven's entrance, the Bible says the gates of pearl will always be open: they "will never be shut by day—and there will be no night there" (Revelation 21:22–25). The gates, made of a single pearl, will be entered by the redeemed in the eternal state: "Nothing unclean will ever enter it, nor anyone who does what is detestable or false, but only those who are written in the Lamb's book of life" (Revelation 21:26–27).

The promise of entry to the New Jerusalem is both beautiful and daunting. The idea of such a city is wonderful to think about—a place where nothing false or unclean or harmful will ever be able to enter. And the pearly gates will be a dazzling sight. However, we have all done bad things and told lies.

Does this mean that we will not be able to enter the New Jerusalem? The answer is "it depends." We are all sinners, but those whose sin is forgiven by the blood of Christ are named in the Lamb's book of life. "Blessed is the one whose transgressions are forgiven, whose sins are covered" (Psalm 32:1). Those who are in Christ are the children of God (John 1:12) and will receive an eternal inheritance (1 Peter 1:4).

What Is Heaven Like?

As previously discussed, heaven is a real place described in the Bible. The word "heaven" is found 276 times in the New Testament alone. Scripture refers to three heavens. The apostle Paul was "caught up to the third heaven," but he was prohibited from revealing what he experienced there (2 Corinthians 12:1-9).

If a third heaven exists, there must also be two other heavens. The first is most frequently referred to in the Old Testament as the "sky" or the "firmament." This is the heaven that contains clouds, the area that birds fly through. The second heaven is interstellar/outer space, which is the abode of the stars, planets, and other celestial objects (Genesis 1:14-18).

The third heaven, the location of which is not revealed, is the dwelling place of God. Jesus promised to prepare a place for true Christians in heaven (John 14:2). Heaven is also the destination of Old Testament saints who died trusting God's promise of the Redeemer (Ephesians 4:8). Whoever believes in Christ shall never perish but have eternal life (John 3:16).

The apostle John was privileged to see and report on the heavenly city (Revelation 21:10-27). John witnessed that heaven (the new earth) possesses the "glory of God" (Revelation 21:11), the very presence of God. Because heaven has no night and the Lord himself is the light, the sun and moon are no longer needed (Revelation 22:5).

The city is filled with the brilliance of costly stones and crystal-clear jasper. Heaven has twelve gates (Revelation 21:12) and twelve foundations (Revelation 21:14). The paradise of the Garden of Eden is restored: the river of the water of life flows freely and the tree of life is available once again, yielding fruit monthly with leaves that "heal the nations" (Revelation 22:1-2). However eloquent John was in his description of heaven, the reality of heaven is beyond the ability of finite man to describe (1 Corinthians 2:9).

Heaven is a place of "No Mores." There will be no more tears, no more pain, and no more sorrow (Revelation 21:4). There will be no more separation, because death will be conquered (Revelation 20:6). The best thing about heaven is the presence of our Lord and Savior (1 John 3:2). We will be face to face with the Lamb of God who loved us and sacrificed himself so that we can enjoy his presence in heaven for eternity.

Where Is Heaven Located?

There are no verses that give us a geographical location. The short answer to this question is, "heaven is where God is." The place referred to in this question is called the "third heaven" and "paradise" in 2 Corinthians 12:1-4, where the apostle Paul tells of a living man who was "caught up" to heaven and was unable to describe it. The Greek word translated "caught up" is also used in 1 Thessalonians 4:17 in describing the rapture, wherein believers will be caught up to be with the Lord.

Other verses indicating heaven to be "above" the earth" are numerous. At the Tower of Babel, God says, "Come, let us go down" (Genesis 11:7) Heaven is described as "high above the earth" in Psalm 103:11, and the place from which the Lord "looks down" in Psalm 14:2. Jesus is described as having "ascended into heaven" and "descended from heaven" in John 3:13 (ESV). In Acts 1:9–11 Jesus is described as being taken "up" into heaven, and when God takes John to heaven in Revelation 4:1, He says, "Come up here." These passages have led to the conclusion that heaven is beyond the earth's airspace and beyond the stars.

However, since God is spirit, "heaven" cannot signify a place remote from us which he inhabits. The Greek gods were thought of as spending most of their time far away from earth in sort of a celestial equivalent of the Bahamas, but the God of the Bible is not like this. He is always near us when we call on him (James 4:8), and we are encouraged to "draw near" to him (Hebrews 10:1, 22). Granted, the "heaven" where saints and angels dwell has to be thought of as a sort of locality, because saints and angels, as God's creatures, exist in space and time. But when the Creator is said to be "in heaven," the thought is that he exists on a different plane from us, rather than in a different place.

That God in heaven is always near to his children on earth is something the Bible expresses throughout. The New Testament mentions heaven with considerable frequency. Yet, even with this frequency, detailed description of its location is missing.

Perhaps God has intentionally covered its location in mystery, for it is more important for us to focus on the God of heaven than the description or location of his dwelling. It is more important to know the "why" and the "who" than the "where." The New Testament focuses on the purpose of heaven and who is there instead of telling us exactly what it is like or where it is. Hell is a place of separation and punishment (Matthew 8:12; 22:13). Heaven, on the other hand, is a place of fellowship and eternal joy and, more importantly, worshiping around the throne of God.

Author's Note...consider this: *"God inhabits the praise of his people,"* Psalm 22:3 Where is heaven located? Is it not in the praises of his redeemed? However, where ever God is, that is the location of heaven. He is omnipresent, which means fully present in every place at the same time. Figure that one out and I will be amazed because God is beyond our intelligence and descriptions.

There is another thing that you might be curious about. If heaven is the dwelling place of all the angels, did Satan dwell there too? The answer is yes. Satan did dwell there until he was thrown out by God.

The scriptures tell us that there was a war in heaven. Revelations 12:7-10 Lucifer, otherwise known as Satan, led a rebellion against God and pulled 1/3 of all the angels away into a battle for supremacy. But Lucifer was not God and did not have the power to overthrow his creator. Here's what happened.

"How art thou fallen from heaven, O Lucifer, son of the morning! how art thou cut down to the ground, which didst weaken the nations. For thou hast said in thine heart, I will ascend into heaven, I will exalt my throne above the stars of God: I will sit also upon the mount of the congregation, in the sides of the north: I will ascend above the heights of the clouds; I will be like the most High. Yet thou shalt be brought down to hell, to the sides of the pit." Isaiah 14:124-15

There was a time, after Satan was tossed out of heaven that he could still approach the throne of God and accuse human beings. Job 1:6 However, he cannot just show up in heaven. He must be summoned by God to appear before him.

There is an assumed motive for his rebellion. Lucifer and all the other angels did not want to worship God incarnate in man. When God said," Let us create man in our image and in our likeness", that made some angelic beings angry. Then when man was given dominion over everything that he created, it was obvious to all that they would be subservient to man and would have to bow to him as Lord. Read it in Genesis chapter one.

But that was not the worst of it. Adam was a prototype. He was to populate the earth with more human beings that would also be in the image and likeness of God and continue Adams dominion, thus creating not just one but millions that would be greater in stature than Lucifer. See Romans chapter five.

Remember, Jesus was the slain Lamb of God before the foundation of the world. Revelation 13:8 This God-man relationship was not common knowledge among the host of heaven or the princes of this world. They all found out when, as the apostle John recorded in his gospel, chapter one, "The Word became flesh."

Hear what the scriptures say, "But we speak the wisdom of God in a mystery, even the hidden wisdom, which God ordained before the world unto our glory: Which none of the princes of this world knew: for had they known it, they would not have crucified the Lord of glory. I Corinthians 2:7-8

CHAPTER TWO:
DOES HELL REALLY EXIST?

Hell is a literal place, just like Heaven is a literal place. They both play a big part in man's future. For the redeemed; heaven is waiting, for the lost or unsaved, hell is their final destination.

According to Gallup research, 94% of U.S. adults believe in God or a universal spirit;

84% believe Jesus Christ is God or the Son of God; and 53% believe in a literal hell.

A Newsweek poll found that 94% of Americans believe in God; 77% believe in a heaven; 76% think they have a good or excellent chance of getting there. 58% of those surveyed believe in hell.

According to church historian Martin Marty, hell began to disappear from man's thinking in the 19th century, and no one seemed to notice. In rejecting heaven and hell, one also rejects the awesome seriousness of moral and immoral behavior. But for those who take God seriously, human freedom means the capacity to make moral decisions, which have radical and enduring consequences.

In general, more adults in the U.S. believe in hell now than they did 40 years ago. The concept was losing ground as recently as 1980 when just over half of those surveyed said they believed in hell. By 1990 the percentage had risen to 60%. One 2011 survey reported only 52% believed in hell.

Mathew 7:13-14 records Jesus saying, *"Enter ye in at the strait gate:*

for wide is the gate, and broad is the way, that leadeth to destruction, and many there be which go in thereat: Because strait is the gate, and narrow is the way, which leadeth unto life, and few there be that find it." (KJV)

There are only two roads in life, one leads to hell, characterized by destruction and the other road leads to life or heaven. The masses, all the religions that do not accept Jesus as the only way, walk down the broad road. It is wide enough for all to fit. But the road to life is narrow…One Way…Jesus, the Christ of God.

Hell is a reality; a real place for real people. It is so bad that Jesus told the crowd in one of his sermons, *"Wherefore if thy hand or thy foot offend thee, cut them off, and cast them from thee: it is better for thee to enter into life halt or maimed, rather than having two hands or two feet to be cast into everlasting fire. And if thine eye offends thee, pluck it out, and cast it from thee: it is better for thee to enter into life with one eye, rather than having two eyes to be cast into hell fire".* (Mathew 18:8-9),

Here are some other references concerning the reality of hell.

Mathew 10:28 *"And fear not them which kill the body, but are not able to kill the soul: but rather fear him which is able to destroy both soul and body in hell."* (KJV)

Rev. 20:10 *"And the devil that deceived them was cast into the lake of fire and*

brimstone, where the beast and the false prophet are, and shall be tormented day and night for ever and ever." (KJV)

Mathew 25:46 *"And these shall go away into everlasting punishment: but the righteous into life eternal."* KJV)

Mathew 25:41, *"Then shall he say also unto them on the left hand, depart from me, ye cursed, into everlasting fire, prepared for the devil and his angels:"* (KJV)

In our modern vernacular, hell signifies a place of fire and punishment and this is indeed taught in the scriptures.

Hell is mentioned in the Bible (KJV) 54 times. Hell appears 31 times in the Old Testament and 23 in the New Testament. In the OT, hell is translated from the Hebrew word "Sheol." In the NT, hell was translated from three words, Tartaroo, Hades and Gehenna. All words express some or all of these characteristics: an eternal separation from God, a place of darkness, suffering, pain and torment. It is not a place where you want to visit or move to.

In my earlier days, we used to say, flippantly, that we'd probably end up in hell, having a party with all our friends. I have since come to my senses, realizing that hell is a place of isolation. Those that go there will be alone with their thoughts forever. Can you imagine being in total darkness, all alone with just your suffering and pain to keep you company? Don't think that your punishment will be administered by demons or the devil. They will be cast into the lake of fire. There are no jailors to talk to or to call out to…just you, all alone, suffering forever.

Many people are uncomfortable, to say the least, with the idea of an eternal hell. This discomfort, though, is often the result of an incomplete understanding of three things: the nature of God, the nature of man, and the nature of sin.

As fallen sinful human beings, the nature of God is a difficult concept for us to grasp. We tend to see God as a kind, merciful being whose love for us overrides and overshadows all his other attributes. Of course, God is loving, kind, and merciful, but he is first and foremost a holy and righteous God. So holy is he that he cannot tolerate sin. He is a God whose anger burns against the wicked and disobedient (Isaiah 5:25; Hosea 8:5; Zechariah 10:3). He is not only a loving God—He is love itself!

But the Bible also tells us that he hates all manner of sin (Proverbs 6:16-19). And while he is merciful, there are limits to his mercy. "Seek the LORD while he may be found; call on him while he is near. Let the wicked forsake his way and the evil man his thoughts. Let him turn to the LORD, and he will have mercy on him, and to our God, for he will freely pardon" (Isaiah 55:6-7).

Humanity is corrupted by sin, and that sin is always directly against God. When David sinned by committing adultery with Bathsheba and having Uriah murdered, he responded with an interesting prayer: "Against you, you only, have I sinned and done what is evil in your sight…" (Psalm 51:4). Since David had sinned against Bathsheba and Uriah, how could he claim to have only sinned against God?

David understood that all sin is ultimately against God. God is an eternal and infinite Being (Psalm 90:2). As a result, all sin requires an eternal punishment. God's holy, perfect and infinite character has been offended by our sin. Although, to our finite minds our sin is limited in time; to God—who is outside of time—the sin he hates goes on and on. Our sin is eternally before him and must be eternally punished in order to satisfy his holy justice.

No one understands this better than someone in hell. A perfect example is the story of the rich man and Lazarus. Both died, and the rich man went to hell while Lazarus went to paradise (Luke 16). Of course, the rich man was aware that his sins were only committed during his lifetime. But interestingly, he never says, "How did I end up here?" That question is never asked in hell. He does not say, "Did I really deserve this? don't you think this is a little extreme? A little over the top?" He only asks that someone go to his brothers who are still alive and warn them against his fate.

Like the rich man, every sinner in hell has a full realization that he deserves to be there. Each sinner has a fully informed, acutely aware, and sensitive conscience which, in hell, becomes his own tormenter. This is the experience of torture in hell—a person fully aware of his or her sin with a relentlessly accusing conscience, without relief for even one moment.

The guilt of sin will produce shame and everlasting self-hatred. The rich man knew that eternal punishment for a lifetime of sins is justified and deserved. That is why he never protested or questioned being in hell.

The realities of eternal damnation, eternal hell, and eternal punishment are frightening and disturbing. But it is good that we might, indeed, be terrified. While this may sound grim, there is good news. God loves us (John 3:16) and wants us to be saved from hell (2 Peter 3:9).

But because God is also just and righteous, he cannot allow our sin to go unpunished. Someone has to pay for it. In his great mercy and love, God provided his own payment for our sin. He sent his Son, Jesus Christ to pay the penalty for our sins by dying on the cross for us. Jesus' death was an infinite death because He is the infinite God/man, paying our infinite sin debt, so that we would not have to pay it in hell for eternity (2 Corinthians 5:21).

If we confess our sin and place our faith in Christ, asking for God's forgiveness based on Christ's sacrifice, we are saved, forgiven, cleansed, and promised an eternal home in heaven. God loved us so much that He provided the means for our salvation, but if we reject his gift of eternal life, we will face the eternal consequences of that decision.

Many people struggle with the justice of that. They question how it is just for God to punish a person for eternity in response to only a human lifetime of 70, 80, 90, or even 100 years of sin. How does a sinner's finite lifespan merit an infinitely of punishment?

There are two Biblical principles that clearly declare eternity in hell to be the just punishment for sin, no matter how long one's earthly life lasted.

First, the Bible declares that all sin is ultimately against God (Psalm 51:4). The extent of the punishment depends, in part, on the target of the crime. In a human court of law, a physical assault against an individual will usually result in a fine and possibly some time in jail. In contrast, a physical assault against the president or prime minister of a country will likely result in a lifetime in prison. And this is the case despite the fact that the crime was a one-time offense, not a continual, ongoing action. God is infinitely higher and greater than any human being. How much more are our crimes worthy of a great punishment in light of the fact that our sins are against God? (Romans 6:23)

Second, the idea that we cease sinning after death is not taught in the Bible. Are those who go to hell suddenly sinless and perfect? No. Those who go into eternity without Christ will be confirmed in their wickedness. The hard-hearted will be eternally hard-hearted. There will be "weeping and gnashing of teeth" in hell (Matthew 25:30), but no repentance. Sinners in hell will be given over to their own nature; they will be sin-infected, evil, immoral and depraved beings for all of eternity, forever unredeemed and unregenerate.

The lake of fire will be a place of eternal rebellion against God—even as that rebellion is judged (Revelation 20:14–15; cf. Revelation 16:9, 11). Unsaved people do not only sin for 70, 80, 90, or 100 years. They sin for eternity.

What it comes down to is this—if a person wants to be separated from God for eternity, God will grant that desire. Believers are those who say to God, "Your will be done." Unbelievers are those to whom God says, "Your will be done." The will of the unsaved is to reject salvation through Jesus Christ and remain in sin; God will honor that decision and its consequences, for eternity.

Why would God do this to me? you might say… because you rejected the only way to him, Jesus. He made the way possible by sending Jesus to die for your sins so you could be free to worship him. He allowed you to live this long and has constantly called you to himself in a variety of ways, all with no response. You sidestepped his invitation, ignored his call and refused to accept his destiny for you.

However, God does not send anyone to hell. They chose not to be with him and hell is the only other place. The rich man lifted up his eyes in hell, in torment when he died and so will you if you reject so great a salvation. **Luke 16:23**

Have I scared you? I hope so because it is no laughing matter. Your eternal destiny is at stake and I want you to know the reality of hell and hopefully keep you from going there…so, here's what you do… *"And they said, believe on the Lord Jesus Christ, and thou shalt be saved"* (Acts 16:31).

Let's take a tour of the scriptures and read what it says about hell.

Who Will End Up In Hell?

Revelation 21:8 KJV But the fearful, and unbelieving, and the abominable, and murderers, and whoremongers, and sorcerers, and idolaters, and all liars, shall have their part in the lake which burns with fire and brimstone: which is the second death.

How Can We Avoid Hell?

Matthew 5:29-30 KJV And if thy right eye offends thee, pluck it out, and cast it from thee: for it is profitable for thee that one of thy members should perish, and not that thy whole body should be cast into hell. And if thy right hand offends thee, cut it off, and cast it from thee: for it is profitable for thee that one of thy members should perish, and not that thy whole body should be cast into hell.

Matthew 7:13 KJV Enter ye in at the strait gate: for wide is the gate, and broad is the way, that leadeth to destruction, and many there be which go in thereat:

Romans 8:1-2 KJV There is therefore now no condemnation to them which are in Christ Jesus, who walk not after the flesh, but after the Spirit. For the law of the Spirit of life in Christ Jesus hath made me free from the law of sin and death.

Why Do We Have To Die?

Romans 6:23 KJV For the wages of sin is death; but the gift of God is eternal life through Jesus Christ our Lord. (see Romans Chapter five for more details.)

Why Do Folks Have To Go To Hell?

2 Thessalonians 1:6-9 KJV And to you who are troubled, rest with us, when the Lord Jesus shall be revealed from heaven with his mighty angels, in flaming fire taking vengeance on them that know not God, and that obey not the gospel of our Lord Jesus Christ: Who shall be punished with everlasting destruction from the presence of the Lord, and from the glory of his power;

Who Are The Damned of God?

"For the wrath of God is revealed from heaven against all ungodliness and unrighteousness of men, who hold the truth in unrighteousness;" Romans 1:1

After reading this scripture, it is apparent, to me anyway, that those who hold the truth in unrighteousness will no doubt face the wrath of God.

This book is designed to shed light on these kinds of people. Who are they? Where do they live? Why do they knowingly resist God? Are they really going to be damned by God? What does "Damned" mean? What exactly is the wrath of God?

Let's begin with some definitions so we know the Biblical meanings.

The Bible definition goes like this, "Hell is the future place of eternal punishment of the damned including the devil and his fallen angels. There are several words rendered as Hell:

1. Hades--A Greek word. It is the place of the dead--the location of the person between death and resurrection. **(See Matt. 11:23, 16:18, Acts 11:27, 1 Cor. 15:55, Rev. 1:18, 6:8).**

2. Gehenna--A Greek word. It was the place where dead bodies were dumped and burned **(2 Kings 23:13-14)**. Jesus used the word to designate the place of eternal torment **(Matt. 5:22, 29, 30, Mark 9:43, Luke 12:5).**

3. Sheol--A Hebrew word. It is the place of the dead and not necessarily the grave but the place the dead go to. It is used of both the righteous **(Psalm 16:10, 30:3, Isaiah 38:10)** and the wicked **(Num. 16:33, Job. 24:19, Psalm 9:17).**

4. Hell is a place of eternal fire **(Matt. 25:41, Rev. 19:20)**. It was prepared for the devil and his angels **(Matt. 25:41)** and will be the abode of the wicked **(Rev. 21:8)** and the fallen angels **(2 Pet. 2:4)**."

What is the Biblical understanding of the wrath of God?

Wrath is defined as "the emotional response to perceived wrong and injustice," often translated as "anger," "indignation," "vexation," or "irritation." Both humans and God express wrath. But there is a vast difference between the wrath of God and the wrath of man. God's wrath is holy and always justified; man's is never holy and rarely justified.

In the Old Testament, the wrath of God is a divine response to human sin and disobedience. Idolatry was most often the occasion for divine wrath. Psalm 78:56-66 describes Israel's idolatry. The wrath of God is consistently directed towards those who do not follow His will (Deuteronomy 1:26-46; Joshua 7:1; Psalm 2:1-6).

The Old Testament prophets often wrote of a day in the future, the "day of wrath" (Zephaniah 1:14-15). God's wrath against sin and disobedience is perfectly justified because His plan for mankind is holy and perfect, just as God Himself is holy and perfect. God provided a way to gain divine favor—repentance—which turns God's wrath away from the sinner. To reject that perfect plan is Love, mercy, grace and favor and incur his righteous wrath.

The New Testament also supports the concept of God as a God of wrath who judges sin. The story of the rich man and Lazarus speaks of the judgment of God and serious consequences for the unrepentant sinner (Luke 16:19–31). John 3:36 says, "Whoever believes in the Son has eternal life, but whoever rejects the Son will not see life, for God's wrath remains on him."

The one who believes in the Son will not suffer God's wrath for his sin, because the Son took God's wrath upon himself when he died in our place on the cross (Romans 5:6–11). Those who do not believe in the Son, who do not receive him as Savior, will be judged on the day of wrath (Romans 2:5–6**).**

The wrath of God is a fearsome and terrifying thing. Only those who have been covered by the "Blood of Christ", shed for us on the cross, can be assured that God's wrath will never fall on them. "Since we have now been justified by his blood, how much more shall we be saved from God's wrath through him!" (Romans 5:9) (Definitions and copy taken from GotQuestions.org.)

What Does It Mean To Be Damned By God?

It is logical to assume that anyone that is under the wrath of God is also damned of God. However, what exactly does that mean? Here's what the dictionary says.

A damned human "in damnation" is said to be either in Hell, or living in a state wherein they are divorced from Heaven and/or in a state of disgrace from God's favor.

The KJV Bible Dictionary says this about the word "Damn."

1. To sentence to eternal torments in a future state; to punish in hell.
2. To condemn; to decide to be wrong or worthy of punishment; to censure; to reprobate.
3. To condemn; to explode; to decide to be bad, mean, or displeasing, be hissing or any mark of disapprobation; as to damn a play or a mean author.
4. A word used in profaneness; a term of execration.

We should never say, "Damn You" because it calls for the wrath of God to be upon that individual and seeks a final solution of eternal damnation. We should not wish that on even our worst enemy. Besides, it is not our job to be the judge, jury and executioner over anyone. That is God's responsibility.

Why Would God Condemn or Damn Anyone?

God has gone to great lengths to reveal himself to mankind. We are without excuse when it comes to acknowledging the existence of God.

"Because that which may be known of God is manifest in them; for God hath shewed it unto them, For the invisible things of him from the creation of the world are clearly seen, being understood by the things that

are made, even *his eternal power and Godhead; so that they are without excuse:"* Romans 1:19

God has a specific reason to pour out his wrath and even damn the souls of men to an eternal death. Here it is, straight from the Word of God.

"Because that, when they knew God, they glorified him *not as God, neither were thankful; but became vain in their imaginations, and their foolish heart was darkened. Professing themselves to be wise, they became fools, And changed the glory of the uncorruptible God into an image made like to corruptible man, and to birds, and four-footed beasts, and creeping things."* Romans 1:21-23

Man has always known that there was a God that created him and ruled over his universe. However, to deny God's existence and refuse to glorify him as God comes with consequences.

"Wherefore God also gave them up to uncleanness through the lusts of their own hearts, to dishonor their own bodies between themselves: Who changed the truth of God into a lie, and worshipped and served the creature more than the Creator, who is blessed forever. Amen...For this cause God gave them up unto vile affections:" Romans 1:24-26a

Vile Affections... The descent into evolutionary paganism is always soon followed by gross immorality, specifically including sexual perversion, such as described in Romans 1:26-29. Ancient Sodom was so notorious for homosexuality that its practice has long been known as sodomy (see Genesis 13:13; 19:4-9). The practice became so widespread in ancient Greece that it was considered normal and even desirable. Other examples are abundant and, of course, it is quickly becoming accepted—even encouraged—here in America. Not surprisingly, this was preceded by widespread return to evolutionism in science and education. (*Institute For Creation Research*)

When God gives up on you, you fall into vile affections and become the worst of the worst among human beings. Here's a list of vile affections: Romans 1:27-

1. **Going Against Nature**...*for even their women did change the natural use into that which is against nature.* Romans 1:26
2. **Homosexual lifestyle**....*And likewise also the men, leaving the natural use of the woman, burned in their lust one toward another; men with men working that which is unseemly, and receiving in themselves that recompence of their error which was meet.* Romans 1:27
3. **Refusal To Acknowledge God**....*And even as they did not like to retain God in their knowledge, God gave them over to a reprobate mind, to do those things which are not convenient;* Romans 1:28
4. **Unrighteous To The Bone**....*Being filled with all unrighteousness, fornication, wickedness, covetousness, maliciousness; full of envy, murder, debate, deceit, malignity; whisperers, backbiters, haters of God, despiteful, proud, boasters, inventors of evil things, disobedient to parents, without understanding, covenant breakers, without natural affection, implacable, unmerciful* (In other words...Immoral) Romans 1:29-31
5. **Disobedient And Rebellious**...*Who knowing the judgment of God, that they which commit such things are worthy of death, not only do the same, but have pleasure in them that do them.* Romans 1:32

I think it's important to understand the meaning for some of the words used in #4 above. Most of us know what they mean but some are not used in today's expressions and may not be as familiar.

Fornication...is generally consensual sexual intercourse between two people not married to each other. ... For many people, the term carries an overtone of moral or religious disapproval. Throughout history, most theologians have argued that any and all forms of premarital sex are immoral. A contemporary example is the modern-day theologian Lee Gatiss who argues that premarital sex is immoral based on scripture. He states that, from a Biblical perspective, "physical union should not take place outside a "one flesh" (i.e. marriage) union.

Wickedness...The state of being wicked; a mental disregard for justice, righteousness, truth, honor, virtue; evil in thought and life; depravity;

sinfulness; criminality. See SIN. Many words are rendered "wickedness." There are many synonyms for wickedness in English and also in the Hebrew. Pride and vanity lead to it:

Covetousness... Strong desire to have that, which belongs to another. It is considered to be a very grievous offense in Scripture. The tenth commandment forbids coveting anything that belongs to a neighbor, including his house, his wife, his servants, his ox or donkey, or anything that belongs to him (Exod 20:17). Jesus listed covetousness or greed along with many of the sins from within, including adultery, theft, and murder, which make a person unclean (Mark 7:22).

Paul reminded the Ephesians that greed or covetousness is equated with immorality and impurity, so that these must be put away (5:3). A covetous or greedy person is an idolater (5:5) and covetousness is idolatry (Col 3:5). James warns that people kill and covet because they cannot have what they want (4:2).

Maliciousness...or Malice," now used in the sense of deliberate ill-will, by its derivation means badness, or wickedness generally, and was so used in Older English. In the Apocrypha it is the translation of kakia, "evil," "badness." We have "malice" in the more restricted sense as the translation of menis, "confirmed anger."

In the New Testament "malice" and "maliciousness" are the translation of kakia (Romans 1:29; 1 Corinthians 5:8; 14:20; Colossians 3:8); malicious is the translation of poneros, "evil" (3John 1:10, malignity occurs in Romans 1:29 as the translation of kakoetheia, "evil disposition"; "maliciously," "having ill will."

Malignity... malice, malevolence, ill will, spite, **malignity**, spleen, grudge mean the desire to see another experience pain, injury, or distress. Malice implies a deep-seated often-unexplainable desire to see another suffer.

Despiteful... adjective. Characterized by intense ill will or spite: black, evil, hateful, malevolent, malicious, malign, malignant, mean, nasty, poisonous, spiteful, venomous, vicious, wicked. Slang: bitchy.

Without Natural Affection... This phrase "without natural affection" is the translation of one Greek word, *astergeo*. It was a characteristic of many pagans of the ancient world. Significantly, it is also prophesied to be a characteristic of the humanistic pagans of the end-times. "In the last days . . . men shall be . . . without natural affection" (II Timothy 3:1-3). These are the only two occurrences of this word in the New Testament.

The word *stergeo* ("natural affection") is one of four Greek words for "love," but it is never used at all in the New Testament. It refers to the natural love that members of the same family have for each other.

It is such a common characteristic of all peoples that there was apparently no occasion to refer to it at all -- *except* when it is *not* present, when people lose their instinctive love for their own parents and children, and thus are "*without* natural affection." One thinks of the widespread abortions of these last days, as well as the modern breakdown of the family in general.

Implacable... not placeable: not capable of being appeased, significantly changed, or mitigated and *implacable* enemy

These folks are soiled, filthy, base, unchaste, sinful, corrupt and polluted. However, Paul says that this portrait, at one time, was a picture of us. We were the monsters that ruled the world in sin. See it for yourself in Paul's letters to Titus and the Colossian church.

"For we ourselves also were sometimes foolish, disobedient, deceived, serving divers lusts and pleasures, living in malice and envy, hateful, and hating one another." Titus 3:3

"And you, that were sometime alienated and enemies in your mind by wicked works, yet now hath he reconciled in the body of his flesh through death, to present you holy and unblameable and unreproveable in his sight:" Colossians 1:21-22

You'll remember that God created man in his own image and in his likeness. Man was, originally, created to manifest the very character or nature of God on the earth. But, with the disobedience of one man,

Adam, sin entered into the human race and death came as a result of that sin...so says Paul in his letter to the Romans.

"Wherefore, as by one man sin entered into the world, and death by sin; and so death passed upon all men, for that all have sinned:" Romans 5:12

"And you hath he quickened, who were dead in trespasses and sins; Wherein in time past ye walked according to the course of this world, according to the prince of the power of the air, the spirit that now worketh in the children of disobedience: Among whom also we all had our conversation in times past in the lusts of our flesh, fulfilling the desires of the flesh and of the mind; and were by nature the children of wrath, even as others." Ephesians 2:1-3

These scriptures tell us about ourselves before being, "Born Again"

1. We were just like everyone else, dead in our sins.
2. We walked according to the lifestyle of this world, following the call of immorality.
3. We were slaves to Satan who rules the souls that are living on planet earth but dead spiritually.
4. We were children of wrath and disobedient against the will of God.
5. We talked the talk and walked the walk as people of the flesh, not the Spirit.
6. We were enemies of God, serving divers lusts and pleasures, living in malice and envy, hateful, and hating one another.

Aren't you glad that I said, "Were?" Paul goes on to say that Jesus reconciled us to God by his own death, as a penalty for sin. He did all of this so he could present us holy and unblameable and unreproveable before the throne of God.

The true gospel message is that God lost his most prized possession, Mankind. He lost Adam to disobedience and self-will that actually led him to attempt to be his own god. That was the same sin that Lucifer, otherwise known as Satan, and the devil commuted.

The difference between Lucifer's sin and Adam's was that Adam was deceived into believing a lie. Here's what Jesus said that later became the Divine solution. He tossed Lucifer out of heaven and into chains of darkness. God, through Jesus' death, resurrection and righteous life, restored man to his rightful place in God's kingdom. God's great love for us was manifested in Jesus.

"For God so loved the world, that he gave his only begotten Son, that whosoever believeth in him should not perish, but have everlasting life." John 3:16

Why did God do such a thing?" For God sent not his Son into the world to condemn the world; but that the world through him might be saved." John 3:17

How can you and I be saved and escape the wrath of God that he will pour out upon the wicked?

" He that believeth on him is not condemned: but he that believeth not is condemned already, because he hath not believed in the name of the only begotten Son of God. And this is the condemnation, that light is come into the world, and men loved darkness rather than light, because their deeds were evil." John 3:18-19

It should be obvious by now that **God sends no one to hell**. He does, however, allow mankind to send themselves to hell by their own choices in life. Our life choices do affect our destiny. They take us down the road of destruction or up the road to eternal life.

This concept is not new. We need only to look at a man that drinks a lot and we can conclude that if he does not slack off, he will become a drunk. We can see it coming.

The same is true when we look at a person who cares not about their eternal soul, lives for today, denies the existence of God and ignores the truths of the Bible. We can say, if they do not repent, they will ultimately end up in hell. We can see it coming.

Hell is not a good place to go, visit or dwell. Be sure you do not end up there. Search the scriptures and hold on to the promises of God. They are hooks to hang your faith on and a sure guide to the eternal blessings of God.

How Can We Avoid Being Deceived By The Devil

There is one sure way to avoid being deceived by evil forces. That is to know their tricks and how they work. Listed below are a few tools that are in *"The Devil's Tool Box"*

The devil, also known as Satan, Beelzebub, The Evil One, The Thief, The Prince of Darkness, The Serpent and many other names has a, "Toolbox" full of tricks and devices that he uses against human beings and especially the children of God.

Most folks are unaware of the "Wiles" of the devil. In fact, over 40% of Americans do not even believe that there is a real devil, only that he is a symbol for evil. (Pew Report)

The Bible tells us about his tricks. His purpose is to snare us with one or more of his tools thereby creating a, "Stronghold" in our lives, from which he can lord over us.

The literal meaning of a "Stronghold" is a fortified armed encampment that can be protected.

A "Snare" is a device or trap that is used to capture a prey. It can be a hunter's trap for small game or a net that is used to catch fish in the sea.

The purpose of tricks, snares, and other tools in "The Devil's Toolbox" is to capture you, and dominate your thoughts and actions with the ultimate goal of manifesting the devil's evil character through you. Hear what Jesus said about the thief, as he referred to the devil.

"The thief cometh not, but for to steal, and to kill, and to destroy: I am come that they might have life, and that they might have it more abundantly." John 10:10

Whatever you call this, "Evil Being" you have to know, without a shadow of a doubt, that he is real and he is after you to steal your dreams, kill any hope of happiness and destroy everything that is good in your life. He wants you dead but not before he torments you for a lifetime.

News Flash

The good news is that Jesus has defeated the devil and he has no power over you but what you give him. That's right, he has to get you to use your own "Free Will" to accept his lie. That's how he takes control. Let's see what the scriptures say so you know that I am not making this up.

"And having spoiled principalities and powers, he (Jesus) made a shew of them openly, triumphing over them in it." Colossians 2:5

Jesus spoiled all evil principalities and powers. That is a total defeat. Then he made an open shew…this denotes an old Roman picture of conquest over enemies.

The evil king and leaders were tied by a rope to the back of a chariot and led down the middle of the city streets in a procession of conquest so everyone could see and laugh at the defeated foe. This is total victory.

Adam & Eve were not forced to submit to the devil when he was tempting them in the Garden of Eden. They had to engage their free will to do what the devil suggested. Take a read:

There's Always A Choice

"Now the serpent was more subtill than any beast of the field, which the LORD God had made. And he said unto the woman, Yea, hath God said, Ye shall not eat of every tree of the garden? But of the fruit of the tree which is in the midst of the garden, God hath said, **Ye shall not eat of it, neither shall ye touch it, lest ye die.**

And the serpent said unto the woman, **Ye shall not surely die**: For God doth know that in the day ye eat thereof, then your eyes shall be opened, and ye shall be as gods, knowing good and evil.

And when the woman saw that the tree was good for food, and that it was pleasant to the eyes, and a tree to be desired to make one wise, she took of the fruit thereof, and did eat, and gave also unto her husband with her; and he did eat."Genesis 3:1-5

The serpent is another name for the devil. He challenged the Word of God and persuaded Adam and Eve that God was a liar, when in fact the liar was the devil. However, it was the free will of Adam and Eve that chose to believe the devil and disobey God.

The Devil's Toolbox

We have already seen one tool that is in the devil's toolbox. It is, "The Lie" Jesus, speaking to some religious leaders of his time on earth, said this…"Ye are of your father the devil, and the lusts of your father ye will do. He was a murderer from the beginning, and abode not in the truth, because there is no truth in him. When he speaks a lie, he speaks of his own: for he is a liar, and the father of it." John 8"44

1. Lies That Kill, Steal & Destroy

How many times have we believed a lie? The politicians promise all kinds of things but never deliver. Are they lying? We believe their lies and then what?

Here are a few lies that the devil uses to cause us to do what he wants.

1. Drugs can't really hurt you. Try some and see for yourself.
2. Smoking is not really addictive.
3. Sex before marriage doesn't really hurt anyone.
4. Living together before marriage is ok as long as no one is hurt.
5. Taking a pen from work is not really stealing.
6. Drinking alcohol is ok. It's cool.
7. Same sex unions are good because it's in their DNA to be that way.

Now let's look at some other lies that are active in modern societies.

2. Ideology That Contradicts Bible Truth

The way you think is the basis for how you act and the way you live your life. There are certain lies that seek to alter your thought processes thereby changing your viewpoint. Here are a few:

There Is Only One True Church.

All the others are false. You must belong to our church in order to be saved. We are the true church of God.

This ideology is so untrue. Salvation does not come as a result of a church membership. Nor does it come from a, "True Religion" It comes from the finished work of Jesus Christ on the cross. He paid the price of sin with his own blood/death.

Hear what the scriptures say…"Much more then, having now been justified by his blood, we shall be saved from the wrath of God through him. For if while we were enemies we were reconciled to God through the death of his Son, much more, having been reconciled, we shall be saved by his life. And not only this, but we also exult in God through our Lord Jesus Christ, through whom we have now received the reconciliation." Romans 5:9-11

You Don't Have To Believe In Jesus To Attain Eternal Life.

The truth is, you do have to believe in Jesus to be saved and will not see heaven unless you accept him as Savior and Lord. Hear what was said to the people of Israel.

"Be it known unto you all, and to all the people of Israel, that by the name of Jesus Christ of Nazareth, whom ye crucified, whom God raised from the dead, even by him doth this man stand here before you whole. This is the stone, which was set at naught of you builders, which is become the head of the corner. Neither is there salvation in any other: for there is none other name under heaven given among men, whereby we must be saved." Acts 4:10-12

We Are All Children of God

Listen again to the scriptures. They reveal the truth. "For as many as are led by the Spirit of God, they are the sons of God. For ye have not received the spirit of bondage again to fear; but ye have received the Spirit of adoption, whereby we cry, Abba, Father. **The Spirit itself bears witness with our spirit, that we are the children of God:"** Romans 8:14

If I Try To Be Good, That's Enough, Right?

The Bible tells us that even religious leaders will not see God's kingdom unless they are, "Born Again" We must be, "Born Again" in order to see God's Kingdom. That's what Jesus said. Keep reading for the proof text.

"There was a man of the Pharisees, named Nicodemus, a ruler of the Jews: The same came to Jesus by night, and said unto him, Rabbi, we know that thou art a teacher come from God: for no man can do these miracles that thou doest, except God be with him. Jesus answered and said unto him, Verily, verily, I say unto thee, **except a man be born again, he cannot see the kingdom of God."** John 3:3

There Are Many Ways To Heaven.

The lie is that we're all climbing the same mountain but by different paths. In other words, there are many ways to attain eternal life. This is in direct contrast to what Jesus said. Listen... "Enter ye in at the strait gate: for wide is the gate, and broad is the way, that leadeth to destruction, and many there be which go in thereat:" Matthew 7:13 The narrow gate is Jesus. He said Himself that...well, read it for yourself...

"Let not your heart be troubled: ye believe in God, believe also in me. In my Father's house are many mansions: if it were not so, I would have told you. I go to prepare a place for you. And if I go and prepare a place for you, I will come again, and receive you unto myself; that where I am, there ye may be also. And whither I go ye know, and the way ye know.

Thomas saith unto him, Lord, we know not whither thou go; and how can we know the way? Jesus saith unto him, **I am the way, the truth, and the life: no man cometh unto the Father, but by me."** John 14:6

3. False Religions That Teaches Heresy

How often have you heard someone say. "It doesn't matter what religion you follow. You'll still end up in heaven." This lie extends to multi culturalism as well. People say it doesn't matter if you are Hindu, Muslim, Jew, Sikh, Buddhist, Catholic–whatever. It's not a religion that saves us but rather a relationship with Jesus Christ. He must be Lord.

There are many false religions in this world. I call some of them, "Isms." They teach heresy and lead people astray. They distort the truth, deny the deity of Christ and create a bondage that is very hard to break. Here are a few "Isms" to stay clear of. These are Anti-Christ.

Relativism – Relativism is the idea that there is no such thing as truth. The devil doesn't want you to believe in truth because if there is not truth, then there is also no right and wrong, and if there is no right and wrong, then anything goes. He can tempt you into sin much more easily if he can first get you to believe there is no such thing as sin. Relativism is everywhere in our society. It takes many different forms.

Under Relativism I can do my own thing. I can ignore any truth that does not line up with what I think. I am right all the time because there is no right or wrong, just whatever I want. This makes me my own god. How sad!

Utilitarianism – In Short…universalism is a theological doctrine that all human beings will eventually be saved: the principles and practices of a liberal Christian denomination founded in the 18th century originally to uphold the belief in "universal" salvation is now united with Unitarianism.

Here is the melting pot of all kinds of beliefs. You can believe anything you want and still be a member of this church because there is no standard or rule of practice, only what you think is right. The problem is… what we think is right is often wrong and with the devil lying to us; we can be easily misled unless we know God's truth. Jesus said…"Take heed therefore that the light which is in thee be not darkness." Luke 11:35 Jesus knew that much of what was being presented as truth or light was not truth at all. It was actually darkness. We need to stay away from such as this.

Atheism - Atheism is defined as the disbelief or lack of belief in the existence of God. Whereas, Theism is the belief in the existence of a God, especially belief in one God as creator of the universe, intervening in it and sustaining a personal relation to his creatures. This non-religion premise has in modern times become a religion unto itself. It denies God any place in reality and sets man up as his own god. The end of this can only be eternal death. "There is a way which seems right unto a man, but the end thereof are the ways of death." Proverbs 14:12

Mormonism---The Mormon religion, (Mormonism), whose followers are known as Mormons and Latter-Day Saints (LDS), was founded less than two hundred years ago by a man named Joseph Smith. He claimed to have received a personal visit from God the Father and Jesus Christ who told him that all churches and their creeds were an abomination. Joseph Smith then set out to begin a brand-new religion that claims to be the "only true church on earth.

This doctrine is a lie and a distortion of the truth. It is a humanistic approach to religion that denies the deity of Christ, The God Head, The Gifts of The Spirit and many other Bible norms.

Socialism - By the late 19th century, socialism emerged as "the most influential secular movement of the twentieth century, worldwide. It is a political ideology (or world view), a wide and divided political movement" Socialist parties and ideas remain a political force with varying degrees of power and influence on all continents, heading national governments in many countries around the world.

Today, some socialists have also adopted the causes of other social movements, such as environmentalism, feminism and progressivism. They reject religion, faith and are anti-God.

Satanism - is a group of ideological and philosophical beliefs based on Satan. Contemporary religious practice of Satanism began with the founding of the Church of Satan in 1966, although a few historical precedents exist.

Prior to the public practice, Satanism existed primarily as an accusation by various Christian groups toward perceived ideological opponents, rather than a self-identity. Satanism, and the concept of Satan, has also been used by artists and entertainers for symbolic expression.

Liberalism - Unlike traditional liberalism, there is a certain element of tyranny within the modern liberal movement. In past centuries, liberalism was used to literally liberate people from the rule of kings and tyrants.

Modern liberalism is now imposing its immoral beliefs onto people who are not interested in focusing their lives around how their state can help them; it is a forced movement that is functioning more like a tyranny than any other liberal beliefs have ever done. The premise of liberalism is mainly centered in anti-conservativism which rejects moral laws and respect for tradition. The devil pushes liberalism more on the young, encouraging immoral behavior or anything that is anti-God.

Legalism… (or nomism), in Messianic/Christian theology, is the act of putting the Law of Moses above the gospel, which is 1 Corinthians 15:1-4, by establishing requirements for salvation beyond faith (trust) in Jesus Christ, specifically, trust in his finished work - the shedding of his blood for our sins, and reducing the broad, inclusive and general precepts of the Bible to narrow and rigid moral codes.

It is an over-emphasis of discipline of conduct, or legal ideas, usually implying an allegation of misguided rigor, pride, superficiality, the neglect of mercy and ignorance of the grace of God or emphasizing the letter of law at the expense of the spirit. Here are a few non "isms" but equally anti-God:

Witchcraft – This is the practice of magic or sorcery by anyone outside the religious mainstream of a society. This term is used in different ways in different times and places. Witchcraft is part of the Occult that deny God and rejects Jesus as Lord. It is centered in mysticism and preys on uniformed folks that seek spiritual answers.

Jehovah's Witness - The Jehovah's Witnesses are best known for going door-to-door. You have probably seen them in your area, and more than likely they have knocked on your door. They recently spent over 1.2 billion hours in one year proclaiming the so-called "good news of Jehovah and His Kingdom".

Jehovah's Witnesses reject the Trinity, believing Jesus to be a created being and the Holy Spirit to essentially be the inanimate power of God. Jehovah's Witnesses reject the concept of Christ's substitutionary atonement and instead hold to a ransom theory, that Jesus' death was a ransom payment for Adam's sin.

New Age - The **New Age** is a term applied to a range of spiritual or religious beliefs and practices that developed in Western nations during the 1970s. Precise scholarly definitions of the movement differ in their emphasis, largely as a result of its highly eclectic structure. Although analytically often considered to be religious, those involved in it typically prefer the designation of "spiritual" and rarely use the term "New Age" themselves. Many scholars of the subject refer to it as the **New Age movement**.

It is very close to Universalism in that it believes in the spiritual but denied the truth of One God, One Lord and One Spirit, which is the centerpiece of

Christianity.

Islam - "The source of the word, (Allah), who is the Islamic god, goes back to pre-Muslim times. Islam calls Allah god, which is not the God of the bible. Allah has about 1.6 billion followers worldwide. In 2010, Muslims made up 23.2% of the global population. According to the Encyclopedia of Religion, Allah corresponded to the Babylonian god Baal, and Arabs knew of him long before Mohammed worshipped him as the supreme god.

Before Islam, the Arabs recognized many gods and goddesses; each tribe had their own deity. There were also nature deities. Allah was the god of the local Quarish tribe, which was Mohammed's tribe before he invented Islam to lead his people out of their polytheism. Allah was then known as the Moon god, who had three daughters who were viewed as intercessors for the people.

Demonic Suggestions--We could go on and on but you get the point, right? There is a suggestion made by the devil to us that is a lie. It is presented as truth. If we believe it, we fall prey to the devil's manipulation and eventual take over. He wants to be the, "Voice In Your Head" that lord's over you. He wants to lead you away from all that is Godly. All that has been mentioned above deal with lies that if accepted and believed will capture you and lead you from the light of God's glory into darkness.

4. Pitfalls In Personality…The Deeds of The Flesh--Now here are a few inward traps that cause sickness in our bodies and hasten our demise. These character flaws are used by the devil to capture us and take us down the road to destruction. They are a product of our own fallen nature. The Bible calls them the "Works of The Flesh."

There is a full list in Galatians 5:19-21 "Now the works of the flesh are manifest, which are these; adultery, fornication, uncleanness, lasciviousness, Idolatry, witchcraft, hatred, variance, emulations, wrath, strife, seditions, heresies, envyings, murders, drunkenness, revellings, and such like: of the which I tell you before, as I have also told you in time past, that they which do such things shall not inherit the kingdom of God." Galatians 5:19-21

All the devil has to do is to suggest a plan of action that involves one or more of these character flaws and if you buy it, you're off into the flesh that cannot please God. If he tells you that your brother's wife is sexy and you probably could have her and you start thinking of the reality of that encounter, you have committed Adultery. Lust takes over and ego soars and imaginations rule. You don't have to do the act, just think about it.

The same is true of Pornography. If you are just looking, it's still fornication in your mind and that will distort your sense of morality and steal your Godly values. "But I say unto you, that whosoever looks on a woman to lust after her hath committed adultery with her already in his heart." Matthew 5:28

The devil doesn't make you do it. He only suggests that you do. It is your own will that takes you down the road to hell.

The secret to overcoming your own evil desires is to deny them. The Bible says, "Give no place to the devil." Ephesians 4:27 That means to not allow your imagination to see what your heart seeks after. In other words, avoid any opportunity to participate in thoughts or actions that defile your body and lead you into evil. Also, it means, do not give the devil an opportunity to lead you astray.

5. Accusations That Destroy Self-Confidence--The Bible says that Satan, (the devil) is the accuser of the brethren. Here is the exact scripture…"And I heard a loud voice saying in heaven, Now is come salvation, and strength, and the kingdom of our God, and the power of his Christ: for the accuser of our brethren is cast down, which accused them before our God day and night. And they overcame him by the blood of the Lamb, and by the word of their testimony; and they loved not their lives unto the death." Revelation 12:10-11

The, "They" in Verse 11 is us, The Brethren. We can and do overcome this accuser with The Blood of The Lamb, The Word of Our Testimony and Because We Loved Not Our Lives Unto Death. Revelation 12:11 We can have victory. You may be wondering what types of accusations are made against us. Here are a few:

1. You are ugly and stupid.
2. You are not worthy of anyone's love.
3. You cannot be saved because you have done too many bad things.
4. You are a bad person so go ahead and be bad.

Demonic accusations are meant to cause doubt, fear, low self-esteem and worry among other things. However, the scripture (12:11) also says that the accuser against you has been throne out of heaven. He cannot accuse you before the thrown of God anymore because Jesus spoiled his kingdom and destroyed his power. If we are "Born Again" Jesus, who is seated at the right hand of God, the Father, is interceding on our behalf, saying in effect, "He or she is mine. Their names are written in the Lamb's Book of Life. They've been washed in my Blood."

6. Demonic Strategies That Attack Right Thinking--Larry R. Lawrence offers these four demonic strategies that the devil uses to defeat God's children. We need to know what they are and look for them in our daily experiences so we can stop them from hurting us.

Temptation... Satan nags us to act on addictive urges and to entertain selfishness and greed. How can we resist this direct temptation? Jesus used a two-step defensive technique: first, He ordered Satan to leave; then he quoted scripture. You have the right to tell Satan to leave when you are confronted with temptation. There is great power in memorizing scripture, as Jesus did. Scripture power not only intimidates Satan, but it also brings the Spirit of God into your heart.

Listen again to the scriptures..."There hath no temptation taken you but such as is common to man: but God is faithful, who will not suffer you to be tempted above that ye are able; but will with the temptation also make a way to escape, that ye may be able to bear it". I Corinthians 10:13

Deception... The devil has been called "the great deceiver." He attempts to counterfeit every true principle the Lord presents. Although Satan will lie to you, you can count on the Spirit of God to tell you the truth. That's why the gift of the Holy Ghost is so essential.

The devil will try to deceive you at every turn in life. He will try to get you to believe that right is wrong and wrong is right. Immorality is not wrong. It's just different. Abortion is not wrong. It's just a women's health issue. See how it works?

Contention... Satan is the father of contention. He delights in seeing good people argue. When there is contention in your home or workplace, immediately stop whatever you are doing and seek to make peace. It doesn't matter who started it. "Be not hasty in thy spirit to be angry: for anger rests in the bosom of fools." Ecclesiastes 7:9

We do not want to be counted with the fools of this world. However, the devil wants us there so he and the rest of the inhabitants of planet earth can laugh at us.

Discouragement... Satan effectively uses this tool on the most faithful Saints when all else fails. President Ezra Taft Benson (1899–1994) gave suggestions for fighting discouragement. They include serving others; working hard and avoiding idleness; practicing good health habits; seeking a priesthood blessing; listening to inspiring music; counting your blessings; and setting goals. And above all, as the scriptures teach, we are to pray always so we can conquer Satan.

When we get discouraged, it is usually because we didn't get our way. Something hindered us from being on top. Instead, we got fired, lost in a card game, watched as our spouse left us or some other bad thing.

There is an easy remedy for discouragement. That is to make Jesus the Lord of your life and trust him in every circumstance. This takes the burden of responsibility off of you and allows God to work out everything for good.

7. Materialism That Denies The Hereafter--I'm not talking about going to the mall to shop until you drop. That's a minor form of materialism. The deeper problem is the growing conviction that there is no supernatural realm. God, the angels, demons, heaven and hell are just a myth. There's no invisible world.

The church is just an institution of man's making by which he controls the masses. The pastors, priests and church leaders are no more than social workers. Marriage is just a piece of paper, and salvation is not necessary because there is no after-life.

That's materialism. Do you recognize it?

It is anti-God in every way because it rejects any future existence after death. The irony is that this type of thinking makes life a total waste. The fact that we exist has no meaning. If we become rich and powerful or just live life normally makes no difference. Whatever we do is without purpose because it really does not matter because there is no after life, judgment or reward. We need to resist this type of reasoning at all cost. It's a lie. God does exist. There is an after-life. We will be held accountable for our actions.

8. Situational Ethics That Replaces Absolute Truth--This is another name for moral relativism. The idea is that nothing is right or wrong except for the intentions and circumstances of the moral choice. If you mean well and the circumstances justify it, then what you've chosen to do is okay. Huge numbers of Christians have accepted this premise to justify abortion. If it feels right, it must be ok. However, feeling right is not the same as God's Moral Laws. His Word is absolute, no matter what you or I feel.

The devil will always invoke a situational ethic into the mix so as to divert our thinking away from the absolute truth of God's Word. Here's an example of situational sin…We all know that it is wrong to steal. It is so said in the 10- commandments that man shall not steal. However, if I am hungry and have no money and am down on my luck, it's ok to swipe a loaf of bread from a supermarket or a candy bar from a drug store. Right? Wrong! Wrong! Wrong! The situation does not overthrow God's law. It is always wrong to steal, no matter why we do it.

9. Scientific Facts That Contradict Biblical Revelation--This is the idea that the only kind of truth is scientific truth. It's a powerful lie of Satan because it is one of those things, which is simply assumed in society. "We all know that science has disproved the Bible, right?" Wrong. All truth is God's truth and true science is always the sister of true theology. Scientism is an offshoot of atheism. "There is no God. There are just the laws of science. That's all." No! No! No!

This Godless doctrine ushered in evolution back in the 18th century. It was the devil's way of offering a believable platform for those who did not want to follow God. As you may know, this theory says we evolved over millions of years into what we are today, with no divine influences. Thus, we are our own gods and masters of our own destinies. Hitler used this theory to killed six million Jews in WWII.

African Americans were once considered sub-standard beings because of this theory. Hear what the Bible says… "And as it is appointed unto men once to die, but after this the judgment: So, Christ was once offered to bear the sins of many; and unto them that look for him shall he appear the second time without sin unto salvation." Hebrews 9:27-28 We should be looking to Jesus, not science.

10. A "Snare" or Trap That Captures The Unaware--The devil will use anything he can to capture us and use us to do his will. It can be hate, jealousy, pride, sex, gluttony, fame, fortune, power and the like. All he has to do is set the trap, dangle

the bait in front of us and wait for us to engage our free will to go after it. Christians, "Beware!"

11. False Prophets & Teachers That Lead people Astray--Here's what the Bible says about false prophets and teachers…"And many false prophets shall rise, and shall deceive many." Matthew 24:11 Mark 13:22 says it this way…"For false Christs and false prophets shall rise, and shall shew signs and wonders, to seduce, if it were possible, even the elect."

It is clear that the goal of these false prophets is to deceive. Their teachings are false. Their efforts are for self-empowerment. Their doctrines are demonic in nature. Have you ever heard of Rev. Jones that took his congregation overseas and killed them all… but only after abusing the females and stealing their wealth?

Let's bring this on the level of the average Christian who can also be a false teacher. Here again what Jesus said to his disciples…"For many shall come in my name, saying, I am Christ; and shall deceive many.: Matthew 24:5 The term, "Christ" literally means Anointed.

What is really being said is that there will be many that claim to be anointed of God, like Jesus was anointed. This is the mark of a Christian but these false Christians are not anointed. They just claim to be. They will be able to talk the talk but do not follow the truth of the gospel message.

A good example is the Mormon Church. These days they claim to be the

Latter-Day Saints and call themselves Christians. However, they believe very differently. Their doctrines are anti-Christ. These false believers are sprinkled throughout all main line

denominations.

How many folks do you know that profess to be a Christian but have no knowledge of what it really means? Some even claim to be anointed when they operate in the flesh and promote a secular gospel that is a kin to Humanism.

12. Sickness & Disease That Kills The Body--The devil will use sickness and disease to steal our strength, destroy our health and kill our healthy cells. However, we are challenged to believe another report. This time it's not the doctor's diagnosis but the Divine Healer's Report.

The question is, **"Does God Want You To Be Healed"** or **Will He Say No To Your Plea?** I was a Baptist, way back when. Our prayer for healing always started with, **"If It Be Thy Will"** We never knew if it was God's will to heal or not. Maybe there was a reason why he didn't want us to be healed. Then I looked into the scriptures and found these declarations:

Healed By His Stripes

"He is despised and rejected of men; a man of sorrows, and acquainted with grief: and we hid as it were our faces from him; he was despised, and we esteemed him not. Surely, he hath borne our griefs, and carried our sorrows: yet we did esteem him stricken, smitten of God, and afflicted. But he was wounded for our transgressions, he was bruised for our iniquities: the chastisement of our peace was upon him; and with his stripes we are healed." Isaiah 5.:3-6 "Who hath believed our report? and to whom is the arm of the LORD revealed?" Isaiah 53:1

Note: This suffering servant, spoken of by Isaiah, has borne our grief and carried our sorrows. He was stricken of God. He was wounded for our transgressions and bruised for our iniquities. The chastisement of our peace was upon him....**and With His Stripes We Are Healed.**

The only person that qualifies in all these areas is Jesus. Isaiah clearly said that our healing is in his stripes, which were the beatings and burises and wounds. His blood and subsequent death brought healing to those who believed his report.

Healed By The Prayer of Faith

"Is anyone among you sick? Let them call the elders of the church to pray over them and anoint them with oil in the name of the Lord. And the prayer offered in faith will make the sick person well; the Lord will raise them up. If they have sinned, they will be forgiven." James 5:14-15

Healed Through Worship

"Worship the LORD your God, and his blessing will be on your food and water. I will take away sickness from among you…" Exodus 23:25

Healed By The Lord, Just Because

"But I will restore you to health and heal your wounds,' declares the LORD" Jeremiah 30:17

All Your Needs Met Includes Healing

"And my God will meet all your needs according to the riches of his glory in Christ Jesus." Philippians 4:19 **Healing is a need.**

Healing By God's Divine Will

"He himself bore our sins" in his body on the cross, so that we might die to sins and live for righteousness; "by his stripes (wounds) you were healed." 1 Peter 2:24

Healing By Increasing Strength

"He gives strength to the weary and increases the power of the weak." Isaiah 40:29

Healing By The Word of God

"Then they cried to the LORD in their trouble, and he saved them from their distress. He sent out his word and healed them; he rescued them from the grave. Let them give thanks to the LORD for his unfailing love and his wonderful deeds for mankind." Psalms 107:19

Healing For The Broken Hearted

"He heals the brokenhearted and binds up their wounds." Psalms 147:3

All Were Healed...No One Was Rejected

"Jesus went through all the towns and villages, teaching in their synagogues, proclaiming the good news of the kingdom and healing every disease and sickness." Matthew 9:35

The Devil Uses Sickness & Diseases To Oppress The Children of God.

The Bible tells us "How God anointed Jesus of Nazareth with the Holy Ghost and with power: who went about doing good, and healing all that were **oppressed of the devil**; for God was with him." "And when they came to the crowd, a man came up to him and, kneeling before him, said, "Lord, have mercy on my son, for he has seizures and he suffers terribly. For often he falls into the fire, and often into the water. And I brought him to your disciples, and they could not heal him." And Jesus answered, "O faithless and twisted generation, how long am I to be with you? How long am I to bear with you? Bring him here to me." **And Jesus rebuked the demon and it came out of him and the boy was healed instantly"** Matthew 17:14-18

"Now he was teaching in one of the synagogues on the Sabbath. And behold, there was a woman who had had a disabling spirit for eighteen years. She was bent over and could not fully straighten herself. When Jesus saw her, he called her over and said to her, "Woman, you are freed from your disability."

And he laid his hands on her, and immediately she was made straight, and she glorified God. But the ruler of the synagogue, indignant because Jesus had healed on the Sabbath, said to the people, "There are six days in which work ought to be done. Come on those days and be healed, and not on the Sabbath day."

Then the Lord answered him, "You hypocrites! Does not each of you on the Sabbath untie his ox or his donkey from the manger and lead it away to water it? **"And ought not this woman, a daughter of Abraham whom Satan bound for eighteen years, be loosed from this bond on the Sabbath day?"** Luke 13:10-16

Is there any question as to God not wanting His children to be healed? There was no time when someone did not get healed. Sometimes it was because they asked to be healed. Other times God just healed them.

We should never say, "If It Be Thy Will." Based upon these scriptures, we should

now know that it is and always will be God's will that we be healed.

Why Then, In Our Day, Do Many Not Get Healed?

That is a good question. I have prayed for some and seen them receive their healing. I have also prayed and saw nothing happen. Here's what I have surmised after more than 50 years of following Christ.

Some folks just do not believe that Jesus can or will heal them. Some have more faith in doctors and pills than they do in Jesus. Some secretly like their condition because they get sympathy and attention that they would ordinarily not get if they were well. Some get disability checks and do not have to work and like it that way. Some are reaping what they sowed and have to endure it. Some are weak in faith and lose hope before they are healed.

Still others just do not get healed and do not know why. They pray, they cry, they plead and nothing happens. The woman with the issue of blood was bound for 18 years. The blind man was blind from birth so God's power could be used to glorify the name of Jesus. Sometimes there are reasons why things don't go, as we so desire.

This one thing I do know…It is God's will that all of us be in good health and prosper. Until he tells me otherwise, I will continue to seek him for my healing and believe that I have what I ask for. In fact, I regularly call forth healing into existence. It is an unseen reality that is and is not but will soon to be.

Sickness can come upon us from several sources. If we smoke and get lung cancer, it is our fault, not the devil's or even God's. If we drink alcohol in excess and become an alcoholic, whose fault is it? If we work ourselves to death and come down with a cold or get sick, is it anyone's fault other than our own?

In a world tainted by sin, sickness and disease and even death will always be with us. We are fallen beings, with physical bodies prone to disease and illness. Some sickness is simply a result of the natural course of things in this world. Sickness can also be the result of a demonic attack. However, sickness does not originate with God.

The Bible, again says, "The Lord is not slack concerning his promise, as some men count slackness; but is longsuffering to us-ward, **not willing that any should perish,** but that all should come to repentance." 2 Peter 3:9

If God does not want us to perish, that is a clear indication that he does not afflict us with a sickness or a disease that would cause our demise. It's just not logical. I believe I have made a good case against, "If It Be Thy Will". All these scriptures lead me to one big conclusion…It is God's will that we be healed and stay in good health.

13. Expectations That Discourage "Free Will" Choices

The devil often uses people to do his bidding. It could be a parent, co-worker, teacher or even a friend. Their efforts to impose expectation on you can be very painful. It could be an immoral act, a restrictive influence or even a command that goes against what you feel is right.

This type of expectation puts pressure on you to be or do what they want instead of what you feel is right. It is a form of oppression. On the other hand, God's expectations are designed to give you the greatest freedom and blessings. Hear what the psalmist said many years ago, "My soul, wait thou only upon God; for my expectation is from him." Psalm 62:5

If you feel that what others are expecting of you is not in God's plan for your life or that you just do not have peace about what is expected of you, reject it, no matter who it is. Your peace is more important than their expectations. That will keep the devil at bay and you free. We should always look for what God would expect of us and reject the expectations of others. By the way, God's expectations are clearly revealed in the Bible.

14. Illusions & Mind Games That Confuse And Manipulate

The devil will also use illusions to confuse you or cause you to think that he has power over you or cause you to think that he owns the world and even people in it. Listen to how he tried to trick Jesus…

"The devil said to him, (Jesus), "I will give you all the power and glory of these kingdoms. All of it has been given to me, and I give it to anyone I please." Luke 4:6

The devil did not own the kingdoms of the world. Nor did he have the power and glory of those kingdoms. They belong to God. "The earth is the LORD's, and the fullness thereof; the world, and they that dwell therein. For he hath founded it upon the seas, and established it upon the floods." Psalm 24:1-2

As the story goes, the devil took Jesus up to the pinnacle of the temple to show him all the kingdoms of the world. The problem is, you cannot see all the kingdoms of the world from that vantage point.

The devil likes to play with your mind and manipulate your imagination. He will play mind games with you in hopes that you will engage your imagination to mentally see what is being suggested. It all takes place in the mind and it is usually a bold-faced lie.

Here's how it works with folks today. A thought enters the mind of a kid from the devil or one of his demons. He is in a store looking at a toy truck. The suggestion is, "Take it, no one is looking". The kid mentally sees himself playing with it and sees all his friends being envious of him because he has the new truck and they do not… so he steals it.

It could be a lonely guy wishing he could find a girl. Suddenly a thought enters his mind. It's of an old girlfriend. Another thought tells him, "Boy I could really …you can fill in the rest. Now he is mentally engaged in a sexual act that is not real…thus, he falls into sin, gets depressed because he realizes he is still alone, hates himself for thinking that way and becomes suicidal.

The devil will always suggest that you picture things that you don't or cannot have. He does this because it is tormenting and he loves to torment us as he takes us down the road to hell. His ultimate goal is to drive you to a place where you will act out your fantasies. Thus, comes rape, murder, watching pornography and all the deeds of the flesh listed in Galatians chapter five.

The thing to realize is…not all of our thoughts are ours. We get some from the devil, from our own sinful nature and even some from the Holy Spirit. We have to try the spirits to be sure they are from God before we act on them. Hear what the apostle John says…"Beloved, believe not every spirit, but try the spirits whether they are of God: because many false prophets are gone out into the world. Hereby know ye the

Spirit of God: Every spirit that confesses that Jesus Christ is come in the flesh is of God: And every spirit that confesses not that Jesus Christ is come in the flesh is not of God: and this is that spirit of antichrist, whereof ye have heard that it should come; and even now already is it in the world." I John 4:1-5

Jesus used the scriptures to defeat the devil. He said, **"IT IS WRITTEN." He knew the Word of God and used it to put down the lie and dispel the illusion.**

This means if we want to defeat the devil, we also need to know what is written so

we can use it at the appropriate time. I am referring to the written Word of God, the Bible. If we are tempted to steal, we can say, it is written,

"Thou Shalt Not Steal" Exodus 20:15 This will dispel the illusion. Then we can tell the devil to take a hike.

Knowing scripture is essential to winning the battle. Here's what Paul said to the Corinthian church back in the first century, "For the weapons of our warfare are not carnal but mighty in God for pulling down strongholds, casting down imaginations and every high thing that exalts itself above the knowledge of God, bringing every thought into captivity to the obedience of Christ" II Corinthians 10:4-5

If we know the scripture, we can cast down every imagination that is against the knowledge of God. That is what Jesus did. He knew that God said that man was not to steal and he used that truth to overcome the devil.

Remember, what God did in the Old Testament was then. We are now in a New Covenant where God's grace (Unmerited Favor) rules the day. God does not punish his children with disease or sickness. His loving hand is extended towards all who believe, He wants them all to come to repentance.

I am sure you will find other tools that should be added to the devil's toolbox. I have shown you enough to open your eyes to the, "Wiles" of the devil in hopes that you search out ways to defend yourself. We are in a fight for our lives that has eternal consequences.

The Apostle Peter gave us a clear and present danger with an assurance of victory.

Here's what he said, "Be sober, be vigilant; because your adversary the devil, as a roaring lion, walketh about, seeking whom he may devour: Whom resist steadfast in the faith, knowing that the same afflictions are accomplished in your brethren that are in the world." I Peter 5:8-9

The Apostle Paul said this about that, "For the weapons of our warfare are not carnal, but mighty through God to the pulling down of strong holds;) Casting down imaginations, and every high thing that exalts itself against the knowledge of God, and bringing into captivity every thought to the obedience of Christ" 2 Corinthians 10:4-5

CHAPTER THREE:
BEYOND HEAVEN AND HELL

We have looked at Heaven and Hell as places for the dead. However, those in hell are really dead and those in heaven are not dead. They died and no longer are alive on earth but they are alive in God. Their physical death was only a transformation that put them in the loving arms of God the Father.

We did not discuss the great tribulation, the rapture of the church, the final battle on earth where Satan is captured and bound in a bottomless pit for 1,000 years and other events that have yet to take place. These are stepping stones leading up to final judgment and the fulfillment of everyone's destiny. That's another book for me to write in the future.

We looked at Heaven. Then we looked at Hell. Now it is time to look beyond them both to see what is in store for humanity. In doing so, we will also discover our own destiny.

We do not know exactly what the future holds. However, we do know some things that are clearly stated in the Bible.

1. We cannot even imagine the splendor and beauty of that which God has in store for us. "But as it is written, Eye hath not seen, nor ear heard, neither have entered into the heart of man, the things which God hath prepared for them that love him." Read full chapter. 1 Corinthians 2:9

We do know that we will be in the presence of God, the Father and that

Jesus went away after his resurrection to prepare a place for us. These two things in themselves makes eternity worthwhile.

Imagine…God is Love and we will be in his presence basking in his perfect love forever. That sounds ok to me. Then somewhere along the line we will have a home in heaven. Jesus said that there are many mansions. Maybe one of them has your name on it.

2. There will be a new heaven and a new earth. "Then I saw a new heaven and a new earth, for the first heaven and the first earth had passed away, and there was no longer any sea. "Revelation 21:1

If there is a new heaven and a new earth in our future, what will they be like? Will there be rainbows and warm sunlight or will Jesus provide the light that shines out from his glorified body? "The sun shall be no more thy light by day; neither for brightness shall the moon give light unto thee: but the Lord shall be unto thee an everlasting light, and thy God thy glory. Thy sun shall no longer go down; neither shall thy moon withdraw itself: for the Lord shall be thine everlasting light, and the days of thy mourning shall be ended." Isaiah 60:19-20

What happens to the old heaven and the old earth? "But the heavens and the earth, which are now, by the same word are kept in store, reserved unto fire against the day of judgment and perdition of ungodly men." II Peter 3:7

"But the day of the Lord will come as a thief in the night; in the which the heavens shall pass away with a great noise, and the elements shall melt with fervent heat, the earth also and the works that are therein shall be burned up." II Peter 3: 10 "Looking for and hasting unto the coming of the day of God, wherein the heavens being on fire shall be dissolved, and the elements shall melt with fervent heat?" II Peter 3:12

3. God's kingdom will come on earth as it is in heaven. "I saw the Holy City, the new Jerusalem, coming down out of heaven from God, prepared as a bride beautifully dressed for her husband. And I heard a loud voice from the throne saying, "Look! God's dwelling place is now among the people, and he will dwell with them. They will be his people, and God himself will be with them and be their God. Revelation 21:2-3

The Holy City comes from heaven to the new earth, not the old one. The old one has melted away.

Remember the Lord's Prayer? Jesus gave it to the disciples as a guide to use when they prayed. If you cannot remember it, here it is.

The Lord's Prayer

Our Father who art in heaven, hallowed be thy name.
Thy kingdom come. Thy will be done on earth as it is in heaven.
Give us this day our daily bread, and forgive us our trespasses,

as we forgive those who trespass against us,

and lead us not into temptation, but deliver us from evil.

For thine is the kingdom and the power, and the glory,
forever and ever. Amen.

Notice that the prayer includes bringing God's kingdom to earth and his will being supreme or fully in charge on earth as it is in heaven. The, as it is, phrase tells us that God will have free reign and his glory will fill the earth unhindered by evil.

4. **The old things that plagued us before will pass away** "He will wipe every tear from their eyes. There will be no more death or mourning or crying or pain, for the old order of things has passed away." Revelation 21:4

The good thing is that we will never ever again cry or be depressed or suffer insults or get sick. All that stuff will pass away leaving us free to worship God and laugh, sing and be happy…forever!

5. **Hell and death will be tossed into the lake of fire.** "And death and

hell were cast into the lake of fire. This is the second death" Revelation 20:14

The best is yet to come with no one dying ever again and hell, with all its evil beings cast into the lake of fire. The lake of fire is not an agent of total annihilation. Jesus said the wicked will suffer forever. "And these shall go away into everlasting punishment: but the righteous into life eternal." Matthew 25:46

6. **The church, (All Born Again Believers), becomes the bride at the marriage supper of the Lamb.** "Then I heard what seemed to be the voice of a great multitude, like the roar of many waters and like the sound of mighty peals of thunder, crying out, (Revelation 19:6-8)

> "Hallelujah!
> For the Lord our God
> the Almighty reigns.
> Let us rejoice and exult
> and give him the glory,
> for the marriage of the Lamb has come,
> and his Bride has made herself ready;
> it was granted her to clothe herself
> with fine linen, bright and pure"—

7. **We shall dwell with Jesus on the new earth forever.** "Then we which are alive and remain shall be caught up together with them in the clouds, to meet the Lord in the air: *and so shall we ever be with the Lord*." I Thessalonians 4:17

Eternity is a long time. However, there is no time in eternity. We will dwell in the now. There is no past eternity or future eternity. There is only now. It will be a great adventure to be loved by and to love our Creator.

I can say that I see life kind of like the apostle Paul…"For we know in part, and we prophesy in part. But when that which is perfect is come, then that which is in part shall be done away. When I was a child, I spoke as a child, I understood as a child, I thought as a child: but when

I became a man, I put away childish things. For now, we see through a glass, darkly; but then face to face: now I know in part; but then shall I know even as also I am known." I Corinthians 13:9-12

CHAPTER FOUR:

HOW TO BE "BORN AGAIN"

I thought it necessary to add this chapter to my presentation because most folks do not understand the concept. I will attempt to explain and clarify the Biblical truth of being, "Born Again"

We will examine the theological importance as well as the process that takes place. We will look at the experience as a life changing event and search for the many benefits that overtake the believer.

We will examine the new reality that makes up the daily life of those who have experienced new birth in Jesus. We will answer the three most asked questions by skeptics:

1. Why is there a need for a 2nd birth?
2. What proof is there that it really happened?
3. How does it change the life of the individual?

Being a Christian originally meant that you were a follower of Jesus, a disciple. It was not a religion but rather a relationship. A convert to Christianity went through a time of repentance, a plea for forgiveness, and an acceptance of Jesus as Lord.

Today, many churches offer a membership and boldly state that you can come just as you are, with no repentant heart, no plea for forgiveness and no need to live under the Lordship of Christ. That is a big shift in theology.

A Biblical Reality Check

Here's what Jesus said.

1. "If any *man* come to me, and hate not his father, and mother, and wife, and children, and brethren, and sisters, yea, and his own life also, he cannot be my disciple." **Luke 14:6**

The Contemporary English Version translates this verse like this, *"You cannot be my disciple, unless you love me more than you love your father and mother, your wife and children, and your brothers and sisters. You cannot come with me unless you love me more than you love your own life."* **Luke 14:6**

2. "And when he had called the people to him with his disciples also, he said to them, whoever will come after Me, let him deny himself, and take up his cross, and follow Me. For whoever will save his life shall lose it; but whoever shall lose his life for My sake and the gospel's, the same shall save it." **(Mar 8:34-35)**

3. "Jesus answered and said unto him, Verily, verily, I say unto thee, except a man be born again, he cannot see the kingdom of God." **John 3:3**

The Pew report tells us that there are a large percentage of evangelicals that do not identify themselves as, "Born Again." What happens to these folks? Is there a different place that they will go when they die?

According to Jesus, to see the kingdom of God, **you must be born again**. We know from the rest of the scriptures that there is a heaven, kingdom of God, and there is a Hell, a place of torment. It's either heaven or hell. Some will benefit and some will not. Could it be that 51% of all Methodists, 55% of all Presbyterians, 63% of all Lutherans, 29% of all Adventists and 29% of all Restorationists will not see the kingdom of God?

The Pew report also says that 15 % of all Evangelicals and 21% of all nondenominational Christians do not identify themselves as, "Born Again" This report also says that 78% of all Catholics do not identify themselves as being, "Born Again".

The Question is, Why Be Born Again?

The question is, are non "Born Again" Christians really children of God? I think it is important to examine why Jesus said, "You Must Be "Born Again." He was talking to Nicodemus, a ruler of the Jews of that day. Listen to the story as recorded by John, the Apostle.

"There was a man of the Pharisees named Nicodemus, a ruler of the Jews. This man came to Jesus by night and said to him, Rabbi, we know that you are a teacher come from God; for no one can do these signs that you do unless God is with him."

Jesus answered and said to him, "most assuredly, I say to you, unless one is born again, he cannot see the kingdom of God." Nicodemus said to him, "How can a man be born when he is old? Can he enter a second time into his mother's womb and be born?"

Jesus answered, "most assuredly, I say to you, unless one is born of water and the Spirit, he cannot enter the kingdom of God. That which is born of the flesh is flesh, and that which is born of the Spirit is spirit.

Do not marvel that I said to you, 'you must be born again.' The wind blows where it wishes, and you hear the sound of it, but cannot tell where it comes from and where it goes. So is everyone who is born of the Spirit."

Nicodemus answered and said to Him, "How can these things be?" Jesus answered and said to him, "Are you the teacher of Israel, and do not know these things? Most assuredly, I say to you, we speak what we know and testify what we have seen, and you do not receive our witness.

If I have told you earthly things and you do not believe, how will you believe if I tell you heavenly things? No one has ascended to heaven but he who came down from heaven, *that is,* the Son of Man who is in heaven.

And as Moses lifted up the serpent in the wilderness, even so must the Son of Man be lifted up, that whoever believes in him should not perish but have eternal life. For God so loved the world that he gave his only begotten Son, that whoever believes in him should not perish but have everlasting life. For God did not send his Son into the world to condemn the world, but that the world through him might be saved." **John 3:1-16**

Nicodemus was a ruler of the Jews. That would be the equivalent to being a Pastor or Bible Teacher today. He was a member of an established religious group. He was seen as a man of authority and having wisdom being educated in the things of God. However, like many religious leaders of our day, he lacked the simple truth that makes a person a child of God.

It's not religion, being nice, doing good works, being smart, and wealthy or any earthly thing. Jesus qualified it by saying **you need a second birth, that of the Spirit to see and enter his kingdom**. This can only happen by believing in Jesus who is the only begotten Son of God. The first birth is not eternal due to sin but the second is eternal because of Christ. (See Romans Chapter 5)

Deception Rules The Day

Sixty-five percent of all Christians say there are multiple paths to eternal life, ultimately rejecting the exclusivity of Christ teaching, according to the latest survey conducted by the Pew Forum on Religion and Public Life.

Even among white evangelical Protestants, 72 percent of those who say many religions can lead to eternal life name at least one non-Christian religion, such as Islam or no religion at all, that can lead to salvation.

Dr. R. Albert Mohler, Jr., president of The Southern Baptist Theological Seminary, called the survey results "a theological crisis for American evangelicals," according to USA Today.

Majorities among white Evangelicals, white Mainline Christians, and Black Protestants who do not believe in the exclusivity of salvation say Catholicism and Judaism can lead to eternal life, Pew results show.

Smaller but still sizeable percentages (more than half) of white mainline Christians, black Protestants and white Catholics who say there are multiple ways to eternal life also say Islam can lead to salvation; among white evangelicals, 35 percent agree. And more than half of white mainline Christians and white Catholics who view heaven's gates as wide say Hinduism can lead to eternal life compared to 33 percent of white evangelicals and 44 percent of black Protestants. Surprisingly, Christians also believe atheism can provide a ticket to heaven.

Forty-six percent of white mainline Christians, 49 percent of white Catholics and 26 percent of white evangelicals who believe many religions lead to salvation say atheism can lead to eternal life.

The Bible Tells The Truth

All of these folks that view the path to heaven as wide go against Biblical truth. Here's what the bible says:

1. *Neither is there salvation in any other; for there is none other name under heaven given among men, whereby we must be saved.* **Acts 4:12**

2. *Jesus saith unto him, I am the way, the truth, and the life: no man cometh unto the Father, but by me.* **John 14:6**

3. *I am the door: by me if any man enter in, he shall be saved, and shall go in and out, and find pasture.* **John 10:9**

4. *Behold, I stand at the door, and knock: if any man hear my voice, and open the door, I will come in to him, and will sup with him, and he with me.* **Revelation 3:20**

5. Jesus said, "Enter ye in at the strait gate: for wide *is* the gate, and broad *is* the way, that leadeth to destruction, and many there be which go in thereat: Because strait *is* the gate, and narrow *is* the way, which leadeth unto life, and few there be that find it. **Matthew 7:13-14**

It hurts me to read about how many people that claim to be Christian are deceived and on the wrong path in life. I guess they believe that their church will save them or their good works or the fact that they are worthy in some other way to qualify for eternal life.

Before we deal with how to be born again…to experience a new or second birth, it is important to look at why it is necessary and why Jesus is the only one that can get us to heaven.

Just," One Way"

It is hard for most folks that are not "Born Again" to understand why there is just one way to God, yet it is true. There is only one way and that is through Jesus Christ.

The Bible is our source to prove that the one-way doctrine is valid. **Acts 4:12** says, "Neither is there salvation in any other: for there is none other name under heaven given among men, whereby we must be saved."

Here's why it's so important. Adam sinned against God and died spiritually. "And the LORD God commanded the man, saying, of every tree of the garden thou mayest freely eat: 17 But of the tree of the knowledge of good and evil, thou shalt not eat of it: for in the day that thou eat thereof thou shalt surely die." **Genesis 2:16-17**

The creation account shows Adam being made of clay and God breathing into him the breath of life. He thus became a living soul. "And the LORD God formed man of the dust of the ground, and breathed into his nostrils the breath of life; and man became a living soul." **Genesis 2:7**. When he sinned, the breath of life was taken from him and he became a dead soul. He was truly the first of a fallen race of the walking dead.

Life is always in relationship to God. It is his breath or Spirit that makes us alive. So, death passed upon all men for all sinned. **(Romans 5:12)** Their nature was now sinful. We see this in all of us and in our society.

The 2nd birth experience is by the Spirit. The Breath of Life is given to each repentant heart and their souls become alive to God. They become his children by birth.

Jesus is the only way to attain salvation. All the world religions cannot save us. Joining a church or specific faith cannot save us. It must be an acknowledgment of our sin, our cry before the throne of God for forgiveness, and our invitation for Jesus to come into our hearts and save us. His name is the only name that can get us through death into eternal life.

Here are a few scriptures that support the "One-Way" doctrine.

1. ...there is one God, and one mediator between God and men, the man Christ Jesus; Who gave himself a ransom for all, to be testified in due time. **(I Timothy 2:5-6)**

2. ...Believe on the Lord Jesus Christ and thou shalt be saved... **(Acts 16:31)**

3. That if thou shalt confess with thy mouth the Lord Jesus, and shalt believe in thine heart that God hath raised him from the dead, THOU SHALT BE SAVED. For with the heart man believeth unto righteousness; and with the mouth confession is made unto salvation. **(Romans 10:9-10)**

The skeptic would say, "You mean to tell me that all the religions of the world are wrong and only Christianity is the one true religion?" Remember, Christianity is not a religion. It is a relationship born out of love between man and the one true and living God. There is no one true religion. Religion, in itself, will not get us to God. It is the blood of Christ that unlocks the door and our confession of faith in Jesus that makes it all happen. **(John 14:6)**

Why is Jesus the only way to God? ...Because God planned it that way. He set the penalty for sin, which was death. *The soul that sins, it shall die.* **(Ezekiel 18:20)** In fact, Jesus was the slain Lamb of God before the foundation of the world. **(Ephesians 1:3-7)**

Jesus himself said, as recorded in **John 14:6**, "I am the way, the truth, and the life: No man cometh to the Father but by me". Christianity states that the God of the Bible is the only true God and salvation is only possible by accepting Jesus Christ, his only begotten Son as Savior and Lord. **II Corinthians 5:21** says, "For he hath made him to be sin for us, who knew no sin; that we might be made the righteousness of God in him."

Validation

God validated His Son as the only way in multiple ways so we could be assured that Jesus was indeed the only way to him. Here are some to consider.

1. He claimed to be the only way as in John's record 14:6 says but validation came through miracles that proved he was who he claimed to be.

2. Eyewitnesses saw Jesus' miracles and validated them as authentic. Over 500 followers saw Jesus, after his resurrection, and watched Him ascend into heaven.

3. The prophets foretold of his coming, where he would be born, that he would be God in human flesh and lots more…all prophetic statements were realized in Jesus, even those like in Isaiah chapter 53 that were uttered hundreds of years before Jesus came.

4. God himself validated Jesus as his sole pathway to him. "While he was still speaking, behold, a bright cloud overshadowed them; and suddenly a voice came out of the cloud, saying, "This is My beloved Son, in whom I am well pleased. Hear ye him**!**"**(Mathew 17:5)**

5. The Apostles lost their homes, wealth, and even their lives preaching the gospel. Would they do that if it were a lie? I don't think so. They testified to the truth and were willing to die for it if necessary. (Read Foxes Book of Martyrs)

6. Thousands of Believers, over several centuries have testified of how Jesus helped them and blessed them.

7. I can personally testify that I have seen the hand of the Lord in my life and communicate with him daily. I know he is the Christ.

The provability that one man could fulfill all prophecies about a Messiah that God himself said would come, **(Gen.3:15)**, and perform fantastic miracles while here on earth, and be raised from the dead, and ascend into heaven while hundreds looked on is astronomical. But Jesus did just that…fulfilled everything that was foretold about the coming Messiah. He had to be who he said he was and therefore is truly the only way to God.

How To Be Born Again

It should be obvious by now that it is essential for anyone who wants eternal life to be, "Born Again." **Romans 10:9-10** will tell us how.

"That if thou shalt confess with thy mouth the Lord Jesus, and shalt believe in thine heart that God hath raised him from the dead, thou shalt be saved. 10 For with the heart man believeth unto righteousness; and with the mouth confession is made unto salvation." Romans 10:9-**10**

Confessing Jesus is to acknowledge his Lordship and openly proclaim your allegiance. There is no secret society. That's why the scripture says, "With Thy Mouth."

Believing with the heart is different than with the mind. When we believe with our heart, it means to rely upon, adhere to and trust in. We are to wholly embrace the truth that God raised up Jesus from the dead after being crucified for the sins of mankind.

The power to save us and birth us into his kingdom as his child is in the fact that our heart-felt belief brings us the righteousness of Christ and our open mouth of continual confession in him as our savior actually saves us.

Remember what Paul wrote to the Romans in Chapter 5. He said, in effect, that Adam was the first man who fell into sin and took the entire race with him. Thus, death passed upon all of us. However, Jesus was the second Adam or man that was sent outside of the pollution of human sinful DNA via a virgin birth to be the spotless Lamb of God and to be slain as a sacrifice for sin to abolish it forever. This is why the "New Birth" is necessary, to free us from the sin of the first Adam and propel us by spiritual birth into the Kingdom of God.

How Do We Know For Sure That We Are, "Born Again?"

"The Spirit itself bears witness with our spirit, that we are the children of God: 17 And if children, then heirs; heirs of God, and joint-heirs with Christ; if so be that we suffer with him, that we may be also glorified together." **Romans 8:15-17**

We who have believed can say that we are his children, without a doubt or any question in our minds. We can because the Spirit of God is continually bearing witness with our spirits. He leads us; He communicates with us; he teaches us and shows us truth and error. **That's how we know for sure.**

If you have never seen the hand of God in your life or heard the spirit speaking to you, you might want to go back to God and repent of your sins, ask his forgiveness and ask Jesus to come into your heart and save you. Then receive Jesus as your Lord and Savior. This is the only way you can be born again.

How Does This "Born Again" Experience Change Us

"And you were dead in your trespasses and sins, in which you formerly walked according to the course of this world, according to the prince of the power of the air, of the spirit that is now working in the sons of disobedience. Among them we too all formerly lived in the lusts of our flesh, indulging the desires of the flesh and of the mind, and were by nature children of wrath, even as the rest.

But God, being rich in mercy, because of his great love with which he loved us, even when we were dead in our transgressions, made us alive together with Christ (by grace you have been saved), and raised us up with him, and seated us with him in the heavenly *places* in Christ Jesus, so that in the ages to come he might show the surpassing riches of his grace in kindness toward us in Christ Jesus. For by grace you have been saved through faith; and that not of yourselves, *it is* the gift of God; not as a result of works, so that no one may boast.

For we are his workmanship, created in Christ Jesus for good works, which God prepared beforehand so that we would walk in them. *remember* that you were at that time separate from Christ, excluded from the commonwealth of Israel, and strangers to the covenants of promise, having no hope and without God in the world.

But now in Christ Jesus you who formerly were far off have been brought near by the blood of Christ. For he himself is our peace, who made both *groups into* one and broke down the barrier of the dividing wall, by abolishing in his flesh the enmity, *which is* the Law of commandments *contained* in ordinances, so that in himself he might make the two into one new man, *thus* establishing peace, and might reconcile them both in one body to God through the cross, by it having put to death the enmity.

AND HE CAME AND PREACHED PEACE TO YOU WHO WERE FAR AWAY, AND PEACE TO THOSE WHO WERE NEAR; for through him we both have our access in one Spirit to the Father.

So then you are no longer strangers and aliens, but you are fellow citizens with the saints, and are of God's household, having been built on the foundation of the apostles and prophets, Christ Jesus himself being the corner *stone,* in whom the whole building, being fitted together, is growing into a holy temple in the Lord, in whom you also are being built together into a dwelling of God in the Spirit." E**phesians 2:1-22 ASV**

Read this again. It tells you where you were or are now and where God takes you when you are Born Again. It is truly a life changing experience.

Benefits That Overtake Us At Our New Birth

The above scripture passage reveals 10 benefits that overtake the believer at his new birth. They are:

1. We experience God's great mercy and Love…verse #4
2. We are made alive to God, given eternal life…verse #5
3. We were raised up with Christ and seated with him in heavenly places verse #6
4. We receive his Grace or unmerited favor…Verse # 8
5. We are brought close to God by the Blood of Christ…verse #13
6. Jesus becomes our peace…verse #14
7. We gain access to God through his Spirit…verse #18
8. We are no longer strangers but fellow citizens and joint heirs with Christ verse #19
9. We are becoming a spiritual dwelling for God…verse #22
10. We are his workmanship, created in Christ Jesus unto good works

that were established before we were saved so we could walk in them…verse #10

We have looked at statistics that show trends and percentages of those in error. We have discussed doctrines like Jesus as the only pathway to God the Father. We have looked at benefits of being "Born Again" and why it is necessary to attain eternal life. We have seen how to be Born Again through repentance, a plea for forgiveness and an invitation to Jesus to enter our hearts and be Lord over our lives.

There is only one thing left to do, decide if you are, "Born Again" or not. If not, go before the Lord and ask to be born into his kingdom. Then follow the teachings of Jesus as recorded in the Bible.

CONCLUSION

There is a lifetime strategy that is embodied in the life of the apostle Paul. He looked at life this way…"Brethren, I count not myself to have apprehended: but this one thing I do, forgetting those things which are behind, and reaching forth unto those things which are before, I press toward the mark for the prize of the high calling of God in Christ Jesus.

Let us therefore, as many as be perfect, be thus minded: and if in anything ye be otherwise minded, God shall reveal even this unto you." Philippians 12:13-15

Most of us are so caught up in the past that we can't enjoy the here and now, much less what may be in our future. Paul encourages us to forget the past and focus on the will of God. He characterizes it as a mark of the prize of the higher calling of God. However, in reality, God's higher calling is to fellowship with him in the Spirit and walk together through life's every trial. In other words, to make Jesus Lord of your life and rejoice in his presence every day.

Heaven's final destination is planet earth. Hell's final destination is the lake of fire. The throne of God is the heart of the repentant believer who has been washed in the blood of Christ and filled with God's Holy Spirit. The battle that currently rages in our souls is really in the mind. However, Satan is already defeated and is now subject to our authority. "Ye are of God, little children, and have overcome them: because greater is he that is in you, than he that is in the world." I John 4:4

If you are failing in your faith and weak in your walk with God, you probably need a new perspective. I hope this teaching has helped to strengthen you and equip you for the days ahead.

ABOUT THE AUTHOR
JOHN MARINELLI

Rev. Marinelli is an ordained minister, He has formed and been pastor of one church in Wisconsin and was the pastor of another in Alabama. He has also been a youth minister and evangelism director over the years.

Rev. Marinelli has authored several other books including: "Original Story Poems", "The Art of Writing Christian Poetry," "Pulpit Poems," "Moonlight & Mistletoe," "The Mysterious Stranger," "With Eagles Wings," "Mysteries & Miracles," "It Came To Pass," Why Do The Righteous Suffer," "Believer's Handbook of battle Strategies." "Hidden In Plain Sight" "The End of The World, From The Beginning, Shadows in the Light of a Pale Moon," "Mister Tugboat" "An Elephant Named Clyde" "Morning Reign" "Times Past But Not Forgotten" "How To Be Happy" and "How To Have A Victorious Christian Life."(www.marinellichristianbooks.com)

John is an accomplished Christian poet. He also dabbles in songwriting, likes to play chess, sings karaoke and goes fishing now and then. He lives in north central Florida where he enjoys a retired lifestyle with his wife and two collies.

GALLERY OF ENCOURAGING CHRISTIAN POEMS

AGREEING WITH GOD

We speak of things that are not,
Believing in them as though they were,
Because our Heavenly Father spoke them first,
Sending them to us in promises that never blur.

We take Him at His Word,
And listen to all He has to say.
We wrap each promise around our souls,
Until what was spoken becomes our day.

We will agree with the Lord,
Trusting that He knows best.
For only His awesome power,
Can provide our souls with rest.

"As it is written, I have made thee a father of many nations, before Him who he believed, even God who quickens the dead and calls those things that be not as though they were" Romans 4:17

Like Abraham, we also have a destiny that God has spoken into our lives. He calls it forth before it exists. Like Abraham, we are to believe, even against hope, that what God said will indeed come to be. (Romans 4:18).

ARM'S LENGTH

I hold the world at arm's length,
That its choices do not interfere.
While it does its own thing,
I watch and wait over here.

My steps must not go that way,
For it's not where I need to be.
The Lord has shown me the path,
That will lead me to my destiny.

The call of the world is strong
And pulls at me now and then.
But I know that way
Is full of sorrow and sin.

I must move on in life
Beyond their beckoning call.
It's the right thing to do,
So I do not stumble or fall.

I will not be swayed or misled
By family, friends or business deal.
Their secret thoughts are not mine,
To consider, to admire or feel.

So I keep the world at "Arm's Length"
As I journey through this life.
My faith in Jesus keeps me strong,
As I walk in His glorious light.

"Love not the world, neither the things that are in the world. If any man loves the world, the love of the Father is not in him. For all that is in the world, the lust of the flesh, the lust of the eyes and the pride of life, is not of the Father, but of the world. And the world passes away and the lust thereof: But he that doeth the will of God abides forever. I John 2:15-17

It is more important to know God and to follow after Him, than to become entangled in life's lustful traps: for if we were to gain the whole world and lose our own soul, how terrible would that be?

DON'T WORRY

Don't worry about tomorrow.
You did that yesterday.
Go on with your life
And remember always to pray.

Ask and it shall be given to you,
But this great truth you already know.
Rejoice and be happy, why? Because…
Your harvest comes from what you sow.

I will say it again and even more,
Until it becomes very very clear.
Tomorrow will take care of itself,
But worry is another word for fear.

Now here's what I want you to do.
Trust in the Lord and be of good cheer.
Drop the worry from your vocabulary
And cast out that demon of fear.

Worry is the flipside of faith. If you are walking in faith, you are free from worry. Why, because faith hopes in God and trusts that he will be there to meet your need.

TWO HOUSES

We built our homes together,
Mine upon a Rock and his in the sand.
He thought his would be all right,
But he was a foolish man.

God's wisdom showed me the way.
And what I needed to do,
But my foolish neighbor,
Never had a clue.

Then the rains came,
And the winds began to blow.
The storms beat upon our homes,
And we had nowhere to go.

We built our homes together,
My neighbor and me.
Mine is still there upon the Rock,
But his ceased to be.

Wise men and fools both suffer,
The storms that befall mankind.
But those who trust in Jesus
Will always stand the test of time.

Foundation is everything. If you build your life on the Word of God, it will last forever. That's why we strive to be obedient to the will of God. We want his destine and his blessings, no matter what the world system thinks or does.

CLUTTER

Clutter keeps the mind confused,
As images dance through the night.
Lost among those unimportant thoughts,
Are the dreams that once shined bright.

An endless parade of fear and doubt,
Crowds the mind to destroy our day.
Ever soaring on the wings of the soul,
Until it has formed an evil array.

But clutter is by one's choice,
Of those who dance to its beat.
Better to face imaginations' due
Than to fall into utter defeat.

Be Quiet!!! Is our spirit's desperate cry,
As we call upon the name of the Lord.
Silence is our heart's desired prayer,
Until our minds are again restored.

"Keep thy heart with all diligence: for out of it are the issues of life" Proverbs 4:23

We make the final choices in life that either lead us astray or closer to the Lord. We chose what enters our hearts and fills our minds. May we always choose the path of righteousness and the way of peace.

THE LORD'S LITTLE TWO BY FOUR

God has a little 2' X 4'
That rest on heaven's windowsill.
He uses it now and then,
When we stray from His will.

Sometimes we need a good "Bap";
With the Lord's little 2' X 4'
To knock out the confusion,
And help us to desire Him more.

The Lord's little 2' X 4'
Is what we sometimes need,
To get our thinking straight,
And keep our focus indeed.

The Lord's little 2' X 4'
Is fashioned from life's every trial,
So we do not stray from His will,
Or fall into an ungodly lifestyle.

"My son, despise not the chastening of the Lord; neither be weary of His correction: for whom the Lord loves, He corrects; even as a father his son, in whom he delights." Proverbs 3:11 & 12

It is a good thing to be corrected by God. We should not fear His rebuke for it is not His wrath, but rather a blessing from His love that keeps us moving on towards maturity.

I FIND MYSELF IN GOD

I find myself in God.
He is my, "Everything"
I know that He is Lord,
My Life, My Hope, My King.

I find myself in God,
Not the ways of Sin.
Nor do I look to others,
To know who I really am.

I find myself in God,
To whom I bow on bended knee.
He alone is my joy and strength
And where I want to be.

"For we are His workmanship, created in Christ Jesus unto good works, which God hath before ordained, that we should walk in them" Ephesians 2:10

Knowing that we are created in Christ Jesus gives us confidence to walk in Christ, as He walked, along a pathway of good works. It is our joy and pleasure to be like Him. In Him we move and live and have our being.

"I AM" THERE

"I AM" There,
At the end of your broken dreams,
Before the sun rises over your day,
Prior to those tear-filled streams.

"I AM" There,
Down that road of despair,
When all appears to be lost,
And no one seems to care.

"I AM" There,
Over all of life's twists and turns,
When tomorrow is all but gone,
And when you are full of concerns.

"I AM" There,
Sayeth the Lord of Host,
To bring you hope and peace,
And the power of My Holy Ghost.

"I AM" There,
To be sure you make it through,
In the midst of every trial,
To bless your life and deliver you.

"I Am" There

"All power is given unto me in heaven and earth. Go ye therefore and teach all nations, baptizing them in the name of the Father, and of the Son, and of the Holy Ghost: Teaching them to observe all things, whatsoever I have commanded you: and lo, I am with you always, even unto the end of the world." Mathew 28:18-20

The Lord is with us always. He never leaves our side, even when we leave His. In every situation, He is there. It's time to count on His presence and trust in His care.

SO LISTEN UP

I write this verse that all should know.
What I have to say is like a seed, ready to grow.
So listen up to all I have to say.
It could be the very blessing your heart needs today.

God has not given you a spirit of fear.
Instead, He has offered to dry up every tear.
He really loves you, even though you often fail.
His love and mercy follows you,
Enabling you to be the head and not the tail.
So do not worry or even fret.
That's why Jesus paid sin's awful debt.
Now go on in life to discover its victory
Knowing that Jesus has indeed set you free.

"For God hath not given us the spirit of fear: but of Power and of Love and a sound mine" II Timothy 1:7

There is nothing to fear except fear itself and that spirit has been defeated on the cross. We now have the Spirit of power and love and a sound mind. He will never leave us or forsake us. We are truly free.

WINNING THE BATTLE

We must use the Word of God
To calm emotions that fray.
For the enemy never sleeps,
Until he has led us astray.

So when your emotions overflow
With feelings like depression and fear.
Know this! If you dwell in that place,
You invite the enemy to draw near.

When your emotions rage
With fiery darts aglow,
Stand in the power of the Lord,
Against its awful woe.

And if you get confused
And lost in the storm,
Put your thoughts on trial,
Rejecting all but heaven born.

You can win the battle
That rages within your soul.
By casting down imaginations,
And breaking Satan's hold.

Remember to focus on Jesus,
Holding the world at arm's length.
Lift up your head above the trial,
And the Lord will give you strength.

"For the weapons of our warfare are not carnal but mighty, through God, to the pulling down of strongholds: casting down imaginations and every high thing that exalts itself against the knowledge of God, and bringing into captivity every thought to the obedience of Christ." II Corinthians 10:3-5 The battle is in our minds and we win by putting our thoughts on trial and casting out all that oppose the knowledge of God. This is true victory.

THE LIGHTHOUSE

A lighthouse is a blessing,
To the ships that toss in the sea.
For it shows them the way,
Until they can clearly see.

The rage of an angry storm,
Cannot hide its brilliant light.
Nor can its awesome furry,
Rule as an endless night.

Jesus is the lighthouse,
For those who have gone astray.
The light of His love,
Offers a new and living way.
Jesus is the lighthouse,
When fear and sickness rage.
The light of His love,
Gives hope in difficult days.

So trust in the Lord,
And look for His light.
He alone is "The Lighthouse",
That guides you through the night.

"I am the Way, the Truth, and the Life. No man cometh to the Father but by me" John 14:6

Life holds many dark nights that are full of unexpected storms. Only a deep abiding faith in Jesus Christ will get us through. He is the light of the world. His light keeps us from falling into confusion, sorrow, sickness and demonic oppression.

THE WAY MAKER

Only Jesus can make a way,
Through the difficulties of life.
He alone is Lord and King,
Over life's sorrows and strife.

He is the "Way Maker,"
When there is no visible way.
He will make the way known,
As though it were the light of day.

He will make a way,
For those of humble heart.
He will clear away the rubble,
Restoring what Satan broke apart.
Jesus is the "Way Maker,"
A friend to all who are lost.
He has made the way,
Paying sin's incredible cost.

The way to the Maker,
Is through His only Son.
He alone is the "Way Maker,"
Until life's battles are won.

"Let not your heart be troubled. Ye believe in God, believe also in me. In my father's house are many mansions: If it were not so, I would have told you. I go to prepare a place for you. And if I go and prepare a place for you, I will come again, and receive you unto myself, that where I am, there ye may be also." John 14: 1-3

The Lord is prepared for any emergency. He knows the beginning from the end and has gone before us to prepare a way that we can follow until we see Him face to face.

STINKING THINKING

Stinking thinking, they say,
Is bad for your health.
For it frustrates life's goals,
And denies happiness and wealth.

A right perspective is important,
As we think about everything.
It will either bring us down,
Or cause us to shout and sing.

What we think about these days,
Really does affect our life.
It can cause us to overflow with Joy,
Or fall into depression and strife.

So don't let your thinking,
Stink all the way up to heaven.
Stand in faith before God,
And get rid of that negative leaven.

"Then Jesus said unto them, take heed and beware of the leaven of the Pharisees and the Sadducees" Mathew 16:6

Someone once said, "We are what we think" The Bible says, "As a man thinks, so is he" It is important to concentrate our thinking of those things that are of good report, pure, honest and that will keep us clean of heart.

WISE MEN STILL SEEK HIM

Wise men still seek Him
Who appeared so long ago.
They come now by grace
Through faithful hearts aglow.

Wise men still seek Him
For He is their "Bread of Life."
A sustaining inner strength
Through times of sorrow or strife.

Wise men still seek Him
The Christ of Calvary.
God's only begotten Son
Crucified as Sin's penalty.

Wise men still seek Him
Jesus, God in human array.
King of kings & Lord of lords
Born to earth on Christmas Day.

"Now when Jesus was born in Bethlehem of Judea in the days of Herod the king, behold, there came wise men from the east to Jerusalem, saying, where is he that is born king of the Jews? For we have seen his star in the east and are come to worship him" Mathew 2:1-2

Seeking Jesus is the wisest thing any man, woman or child can do and when we find Him, it is our privilege to bow down and worship Him. This is our journey, our destiny and our life while on this earth.

THE ANGELS CRY HOLY

The Angels cry "Holy,"
While sorrow fills the land.
For God's Judgment Day,
Is to come upon every man.

The Angels cry "Holy,"
While mankind goes astray,
Rejecting the love of God,
To follow his own precarious way.

The Angels cry "Holy,"
Knowing the terror of the Lord,
When all who dwell in sin,
Will suddenly be destroyed.

The Angels cry "Holy,"
Waiting for all things new,
Born of the Holy Spirit,
When God's Judgment is through.

The Angels cry "Holy,"
"Holy is the Lamb,"
Waiting for the children of God,
To join "The Great I AM"

"And one cried unto another and said, "Holy, Holy, Holy, is the Lord of host: the whole earth is full of his glory" Isaiah 6:3

We serve a Holy God that deserves our reverence and homage. The angels know this and worship Him, but man, because of sin, has no real concept of his own creator.

A HIGHWAY CALLED "HOLINESS"

He places my feet on
A highway called "Holiness,"
That led my soul
To the throne of God.

Amidst the cheers of angels,
I walk, wearing His holy gown.
Onward towards heaven's throne,
While evil cast its awful frown.

My eyes were opened
That I might see.
Both the good and the evil,
That sought after me.

I walk the highway-Holiness
That crosses all of time.
Towards the throne of God,
Leaving this world behind.

"And an highway shall be there, and a way, and it shall be called, the way of holiness; the unclean shall not pass over it; but it shall be for those: the wayfaring men, though fools, shall not err therein. No lion shall be there, nor any ravenous beast shall go up thereon, it shall not be found there, but the redeemed shall walk there. And the redeemed of the Lord shall return, and come to Zion with songs and everlasting joy upon their heads: They shall obtain joy and gladness, and sorrow and sighing shall flee away." Isaiah 35:8-10

What a privilege to walk the highway of Holiness. It is prepared especially for us, the redeemed, and it is protected from the errors of fools and the snarl of beast and especially the roar of the lion.

CALL UPON THE LORD

When your burdens overwhelm you,
Like a mighty raging sea.
Call upon the Lord, Jesus,
And He will set you free

When your heartaches are many,
And life is difficult to understand.
Call upon the Lord, Jesus.
He will come and hold your hand.

When your friends reject you,
Because you follow after Him,
Call upon the Lord, Jesus.
And keep yourself from sin.

When you fall into depression,
As though it were a giant pit.
Call upon the Lord, Jesus,
Who will restore your joyful wit.

When you're saddened by the day
Feeling lost and all alone.
Call upon the Lord, Jesus,
Who will make His way known.

When you are weary and heavy laden,
Tired from life's many tests.
Call upon the Lord, Jesus,
Who is sure to give you rest.

"Hear my cry; oh God, attend unto my prayer. From the end of the earth,

I will cry unto thee, when my heart is overwhelmed: Lead me to the rock that is higher than I." Psalms 61:1-2

Calling upon the Lord in stressful times is o.k. He wants us to cry to Him and then to trust in Him to watch over His Word to perform it on our behalf.

IT CAME TO PASS

Things often come to pass,
But seldom do they ever last.
They come into our busy day,
For awhile, then pass away.

We hear their voices, loud and clear,
As they arrive and while they are here.
They speak both joy and misery,
Some to you and some to me.

We say, "It came to pass,"
Or say, "It happened so fast."
Down life's beaten path,
Comes both love and wrath.

So say goodbye to sad and blue.
To all that is now troubling you.
For things will come, only to pass,
But God's love will always last.

"And it came to pass in those days…" Luke2:1

These are the times of our lives. We live them, some for good and some for not so good. One thing is for sure, that which comes our way, comes only to pass on by. It is not what happens that is so important, but rather what we do with what we are faced with.

Trusting in the Lord and seeking His guidance will always conquer that which comes to pass.

THE WHOSOEVER SCENARIO

    The "Whosoever" is who so ever,
    Not who so won't, can't or will not.
    The story is as clear as a sunny day.
    God offers a new and living way.

    But only those who engage "free will"
    To choose life, faith and obedience,
    Will find salvation for their souls,
    And be cleansed and made whole.

    We do the choosing: to accept or deny.
    That is how God set it up to be.
    He made the call to life's "Whosoever",
    That they could live abundantly.

"For God so loved the world, that he gave his only begotten son, that whosoever believeth in him, should not perish but have everlasting life." John 3:16

We are the "Whosoever" in John 3:16, that one day put his or her faith in Christ, believed in Him and now rest in the Lord's love and grace. We have the promise of God that He sent His Son so we could believe and have everlasting life. How great is that?

LITTLE PRISONS

Little prisons await the man with a lustful soul.
Bars of selfishness and pride create dungeons of icy cold.

Prisons of shame and jealousy fill the heart with utter despair.
Bars that separate from God and those that really care.

Stand back! While the doors are tightly closed;
Taking away your life, to wither as a dying rose.

Beware of those little prisons that trap the lustful soul.
Keep yourself free from sin through faith in the Christ of old.

Little prisons need not to be your fate.
It is your choice, Spirit or flesh to date.

"O Foolish Galatians, who hath bewitched you, that ye should not obey the truth, before whose eyes Jesus Christ hath been, evidently set forth, crucified among you? Are you so foolish? Having begun in the Spirit, are you now made perfect in the flesh?

We should always seek to dwell in the Spirit, that we would not emulate the deeds of the flesh. When we fall short, we create "little prisons" that keep us in confusion and away from the blessing of God. It's time to walk in the Spirit and break the prisons that so easily beset us.

REST MY CHILD

Rest my child, says the Lord.
Take thy peace and be restored.
I have provided, thy mouth to feed.
From the beginning, I knew your need.

Do not worry, fret or even fear,
For, my child, I am always near
To bless thy soul with love and grace,
To be with thee, face to face.

Come, my child, near to my throne.
Do not allow your faith to roam.
For those who will not believe
Can never find rest in times of need.

My Word shall see you through.
My grace I freely give to you
That you should rest, thy soul to keep,
Forever delivered from unbelief.

Resting in the Lord is the best way to stay happy. However, it requires faith and trust in God that he will be there for you when you need him. It's kind of neat to relax when fear and anxiety are knocking at your door.

A WHISPER IN THE WIND

There's a whisper in the wind
That lingers both day and night.
A champion of truth and justice,
By the power of His might.

A word in due season
That echoes from deep within.
A voice out of nowhere,
Reproving the world of sin.

Look there, in the street
And here, by the shores of the sea.
There's a whisper hidden in the wind;
A voice from eternity.

There's a calling from God.
His voice is hidden in the wind.
In a whisper, He speaks to our hearts
With the love and counsel of a friend.

Listen for the Whisper,
All who seek to know.
It is God's Holy Spirit
Telling you which way to go.

"And thine ears shall hear a word behind thee saying, This is the way, walk ye in it, when ye turn to the right hand and when ye turn to the left" Isaiah 30:21

The voice of the Lord is often a still small voice, yet always clear and it never brings confusion. His voice is like a whisper in the wind that brings a peaceful breeze to the heart. The joy of hearing His voice is to know His will and our destiny.

FRAGILE FLOWER RED

As a flower in earthen sod,
I bloom for thee, oh God.
To blossom with the turn of spring;
To be to you, a beautiful thing.

I lift my Fragile Flower Red
Upward from my earthen bed;
To draw light from God above,
Strength and peace and joy and love.

As a flower, I bloom for thee
That passersby may stop and see.
Your fragrance and beauty I am,
Flowered in grace as a man.

As a flower in earthen sod,
I bloom for thee, oh God.
Upward, I lift my head,
As a Fragile Flower Red.

"Be not conformed to this world, but be ye transformed, by the renewing of your mind, that ye may prove what is that good and acceptable and perfect will of God."

When we look to God as our source, we blossom, much like a flower that draws light from the sun. When we blossom, like a flower, we display the glory and beauty of our creator to all who care to stop and look. This is our divine destiny.

Other books by John Marinelli can be viewed and purchased at: www.marinellichristianbooks.com

www.ingramcontent.com/pod-product-compliance
Lightning Source LLC
Chambersburg PA
CBHW020428010526
44118CB00010B/472